W. MacKenzie
Kuala Lumpur
Malaysia.

D1612010

2.4.85.

A PLANTATION FAMILY

A PLANTATION FAMILY

Daniel Green

THE BOYDELL PRESS · IPSWICH

© Plantation Holdings Ltd 1979

Published by The Boydell Press Ltd,
PO Box 24, Ipswich IP1 1JJ

First published 1979

British Library Cataloguing in Publication Data

Green, Daniel
  A plantation family.
  1. Rubber industry and trade – South Asia
  2. Rubber industry and trade – Asia, Southeastern
  3. Money family
  I. Title
  338.7'63'389520922   HD9161.S/

ISBN 0–85115–109–4

Printed in Great Britain by
Fletcher & Son Ltd, Norwich

Contents

List of Illustrations

ACKNOWLEDGEMENTS

It will be apparent to the reader that a great deal of this book is based on letters, diaries, balance sheets and company reports. I must thank Plantation Holdings for making the documents on which the last chapter is based available to me, just as I must thank J. K. Money Esq. for providing me with copies of old letters, pedigrees and family histories. I wish especially to thank Mrs H. F. Chambers who, in a time of grief, so kindly showed me, and later lent me, the family documents from which I extracted the story of General Sir John Wilson and Captain Anthony. I must also thank Michael Brander who reminded me of Samuel White Baker's experiences in Ceylon, and Michael Stuart, that expert on the Scots in India, who knew far more about Professor Cleghorn than I did.

I have, in the course of my life, planted and harvested most sorts of crops, but never in the tropics and never rubber or tea. I have therefore had to do a certain amount of background reading. This is not the sort of work to burden with a bibliography. I must, however, mention the use I made of James C. Jackson's *Planters and Speculators*, John Drabble's *Rubber in Malaya* and D. M. Forrest's *A Hundred Years of Ceylon Tea*. Nor should I forget the Kaimakam's *Prize Essay on the Cultivation and Manufacture of Tea in India* any more than I should overlook his *Twelve Months with the Bashi-Bazouks*.

If this book has to have a dedication then it can only be to my sometimes writing companion the Singing Crab.

> *Little crab, Pretty crab, under my skin,*
> *Little crab, Pretty crab, my crabikin,*
> *How you do dance for me, how you do sing.*

CHAPTER ONE

The Background

'*And their incessant labours see*
Crowned from some single herb or tree.'
– Andrew Marvell: 'The Garden'

THIS book is, as its title suggests, primarily concerned with some of the achievements of some of the members of a widely grouped family that has, for well over a century, been closely connected with the plantations. All families, one supposes, must, if only by the law of averages, produce every now and again individuals who are sufficiently interesting in themselves to be worth writing and reading about. Whether the Money family and its collaterals threw up an undue number of such individuals must be a matter of opinion, though it is probable that the law of averages worked for that family as much as for any other. The book, however, is written on the assumption that even those of its members who were not unduly interesting as individuals became interesting because of the work they did and the setting they did it in. So far as the book is concerned, that work was done in the plantations, which means that the setting, for the most part, has to be in what used to be called the colonies. It should be added, however, that some of them showed themselves to be as much at home in the jungles of the City of London as they were in the quieter jungles of Assam, Ceylon and South-East Asia.

British colonial history has been so well documented that a book such as this cannot hope to discover anything that is new. The most it can do is to recall one particular aspect of colonialism that is in some danger of being forgotten in these post-colonial days, and so serve to remind the reader of the extent to which the British Empire was an agriculture venture. If the family can serve to illu-

strate some aspects of plantation life, and if the plantation industries can be used to outline some of the connections between
colonialism and agriculture, then any wider historical purpose the
book may have will have been satisfied.

The Vegetable Empire

Colonialism is so out of fashion – in the Western world at least –
that only our most extreme political primitives still attempt to extol
or even explain it. The rest of us are now happy to believe that we
have become, in this respect at least, considerably more enlightened
and more moral than our fathers ever were. They were taught to
see little that was bad in colonialism. We have been taught to see
little that was good. Educational changes such as these, on the other
hand, need not prevent us considering one particular aspect of
colonialism that is seldom recognised and yet which has some
relevance to the theme of this book. That is the close, historic and
enduring connection between food hunger and land hunger and
between land hunger and the colonies. Indeed, the word 'colony' is
itself evidence of those connections. It is derived from the Latin
colonia, which was originally used to describe a farm or estate in the
country outside Rome. The fact that this meaning was soon
stretched to include a Roman farm, estate or settlement in a foreign
country demonstrates how natural it was for the Romans, as for
most other colonists before and since, to think of their colonies, in
the first instance, as extensions of their domestic farmlands.

It is probably wrong to attribute clearly defined motives to any
set of colonists. Some of them may have had no ascertainable
motives and became colonists inadvertently. Colonies have been
established through accident, short-sightedness or muddle as well
as through greed. It is fashionable these days, however, to find in
greed of one sort or another the principal and perhaps the only
colonial imperative. Certainly that emotion, whether it was dis-
guised as a civilising or evangelising mission, or was frankly exposed as an unabashed desire for economic, dynastic, racial or
military aggrandisement, had its part to play in the establishing of
almost any colony. But so, also, did hunger and the fear of hunger.
For it seems to be a fixed part of the pattern of history that com-
munities should contrive, periodically, to outgrow their food sup-

plies. Few of them have, at any time, been willing to accept famine as a passing but sufficient solution, just as few of them have considered it prudent to rely on trade as a permanent one. Trade is always a two-way business, which, as we have recently seen with oil, can sometimes involve economic dangers. It is in such situations that colonies, if they can be established or snatched, begin to look perilously like necessities.

Yet, for us, the morality of any colonisation depends very largely on the historical time scale involved. We can understand how food and land hunger were entirely valid reasons for the colonisations carried out by people in ancient or primitive societies. Hunting people, to take the simplest example, must, whenever their game supplies fail, occupy new hunting grounds, whether or not they have to conquer or destroy others to do so. We understand this just as we understand the movement southwards in Africa of the Bantu and in America of the Red Indians. The nomads, whose survival has always depended on the adequacy of their grazings, have always had to erupt into the richer settled lands whenever these failed. We understand this also, and so understand the necessities that underlay the conquests of the Arabs, Tartars and Turks. The Norsemen, entirely dependent on cold soils and even colder seas for their survival, would be forced into their longboats whenever a bad season destroyed the fishing or the harvest. This, again, we can understand as constituting the imperative that drove them out to ravage and colonise so much of Europe from Kerry to Kiev. We may even accept that the contemporary partial colonisation of Britain – for such it is – by Asians and West Indians is more an evidence of land and food hunger in their homelands than it is of an inverted and retributory imperialism.

All of these, then, we can understand as being movements of people obeying historic imperatives that transcended whatever moral codes were or are in force. Whatever the autochthonous peoples they colonised may have thought of the morality of being colonised does not concern us. It is only when we contemplate the comparatively recent and short period of colonisation that started from the Iberian peninsula in the fifteenth century and is only now dying, with a whimper, in southern Africa, that we insist on seeing things solely in terms of morality. For being, by now, almost completely non-agrarian, we cannot allow food and land hunger to provide either reason or excuse for four centuries of European

3

colonialism. Yet in Europe, also, there had been endemic food and land hunger ever since the days of the Roman Republic. Even Britain, a fertile and, until the eighteenth century, a sparsely inhabited country has, according to no less an authority than Sir Dudley Stamp, been overpopulated, judged by the productive capacity of the times, for at least a thousand years.

A book such as this, however, need not concern itself unduly with the relative moralities and immoralities of colonialism. The subject has not been raised in order to suggest that, because there may have been a certain necessity, there must also have been a certain morality in the establishment of Britain's colonies which we now overlook. To make any such suggestion today would be, at the least, imprudent. The subject has merely been raised in order to remind the reader of the connections between food and land hunger and colonialism. Whether it is more or less moral to become a colonist because one is hungry rather than greedy must be left for him to decide. But it needs to be remembered that in post-feudal as well as in feudal Europe, and well on into the age of urbanisation and industrialisation, to be denied access to the land, whether as owner, tenant or labourer, was, for most ordinary men, to be denied access to any reasonable hope of economic security. This was especially so in Britain where, because of the early collapse of feudalism, the enclosure of land, the engrossment of farms and the laws of primogeniture, more people were driven earlier off the land than in any other European country. This was not merely an eighteenth-century development stemming from the Agricultural and Industrial Revolutions, but rather a continuing process that had been at the centre of British politics ever since Tudor times. One may, if one likes, discover in this as much reason for the colonising tendencies of the British as can be found in their undoubted talents for trading, piracy and naval warfare. There were always younger sons, dispossessed tenants and landless labourers enough to power the drive to the colonies.

The British Empire, in short, was certainly a trading, exploiting, plundering affair, but it was also, by the same token, an agricultural one. It was, probably more than other empires, founded originally on a need and desire to acquire land and produce food. It is, perhaps, odd that the British, who are now the least agrarian people in the civilised world, should have had what almost amounted to a natural genius for colonial farming. Perhaps only the Dutch among

4

the Europeans and the Chinese among the Asiatics have an equal gift for establishing themselves successfully as farmers in almost any part of the globe that is farmable. Trade, we are told, followed the flag, but in many of the colonies the farmers followed the flag rather more closely than the traders. It was only in the Asian colonies, where the agricultural land was already closely settled and intensively farmed before the colonists arrived that trade was the first and primary consideration.

Even there, however, many of the traders soon turned their attention to crops and the land. If the existing arable land was already occupied and there was no need for them to produce the standard crops, they concentrated on the untouched jungle and mountain lands on which they could grow quite new crops on a scale the world had never seen before and did not even realise that it needed. They established, in short, the plantations. In this way the British Empire was not only marked out on the map with forts, garrisons, naval stations, trading posts, factories and missions. It was also, and equally importantly, marked out with farms, ranches and plantations, with dams, irrigation networks and drainage systems, with Herefords and Shorthorns, Blackfaces and Southdowns, Large Whites and Tamworths.

Andrew Marvell, who has already been quoted, wrote in the pretty conceit addressed 'To His Coy Mistress':

> *My vegetable love shall grow*
> *Vaster then Empires and more slow.*

He lived in the early days of British colonialism, which is perhaps why he failed to appreciate that vegetables and empires could be casually connected as well as poetically contrasted. It could be less than the truth, but it would be more than a mere conceit to claim that the British Empire was, to a certain extent at least, a vegetable empire.

The Plantations

The word 'plantation' was originally used, in a colonial context, to describe what we would now call a settlement. There was some logic in such a usage since the first thing any coloniser has to plant on foreign soil is men. In the sixteenth and seventeenth centuries, therefore, a plantation, whether it was in Ireland or Virginia, meant a settlement of men rather than an area of crops. Since, however, the settlers were there principally in order to produce crops, the word, by a natural development, came to be applied to the crops themselves rather than to the settlers who grew them. Even that shift in meaning was a temporary one. There soon arose the need to differentiate between two different types of colonial farming. There were those farms, principally in America, Australasia and southern Africa, where family farmers could reproduce, though under different circumstances and on a different scale, the patterns of farming they had left behind them in Britain. But in certain tropical and sub-tropical areas where such patterns could not be reproduced, and where new crops and an entirely different way of working were essential, an entirely different way of farming had to be practised. The word 'plantation' came increasingly to be reserved for this last type of farming.

The Oxford English Dictionary, in fact, gives 1706 as the first date when the word was actually used to define 'an estate or farm, especially in a tropical country, on which cotton, tobacco, sugar cane, coffee or other crops are cultivated, formerly chiefly by servile labour'. The word 'plantation', in short, had come at least semi-circle. It no longer meant a settlement. It no longer meant a farm anywhere in the colonies. It meant, instead, a highly specialised form of agricultural undertaking, normally part factory and part farm, garden, orchard or forest, situated in certain fairly restricted areas of Asia or America, that produced and processed specialist crops principally for export. They were grown, for the most part, in climates and sites where European crops and livestock could not flourish and where European men would have found it difficult to engage in manual labour. They were, therefore, principally enterprises founded and managed by colonists and worked by natives.

There are, of course, as many different sorts of plantation as there are plantation crops, and it is sometimes difficult to decide what is, in fact, a plantation crop. Cotton, for example, certainly is one, while flax is not; pepper is one and mustard is not, while tobacco can be a plantation crop in certain regions and a farm crop in others. There are, however, certain generalisations that help to demonstrate the difference between a farm and a plantation. Like most generalisations, they will not fit any specific case particularly well, but they are worth mentioning because the text will provide frequent illustrations of them at work, and because mentioning them now will save lengthy explanations later.

1. Plantation crops can normally only be grown in certain areas, largely because they are successful only on certain soils, in certain climates and at certain altitudes. The necessary conditions for their successful culture may be found in several areas of the globe or only in strictly limited localities in one or two countries. It is not normal for staple agricultural crops and plantation crops to compete for the same land, since what suits the one will not generally suit the other.

2. Where the conditions on the whole of any one estate are suitable, the planter will, in so far as it is economic and prudent, engage in monoculture, largely because a site particularly suited to a plantation crop is too valuable to be used for anything else. One plantation crop may, however, be substituted for another, as was the case in Ceylon, where tea replaced coffee, and in Malaya, where rubber very largely replaced gambier, tapioca and pepper.

3. Few plantation crops are, in the true sense, food crops, though many of them produce what might be described as food materials such as palm oil, food supplements such as sugar and spices, and food substitutes such as stimulants and drugs.

4. This means broadly that subsistence farmers and small farmers can seldom afford to be planters, since plantation crops contribute nothing to the grower's self-sufficiency. They are produced solely for sale, nearly always in an overseas market. Since the planter proper has to live entirely inside a money economy, in contrast to the subsistence farmer and even the small farmer who may live largely outside it, such plantation crops as these last two grow only become important when prices in the world markets drop to levels at which the planter can no longer afford to produce at full capacity and has either to reduce his operations or stop altogether and put his plantation on a care and maintenance basis. In such cases, the small producer, who already lives very largely off his land and who has no labour to pay, can continue to produce and sell.

5. Since plantation crops nearly always have to travel to distant markets, the planter has to be, to some extent, a processor as well as

a grower. What he produces has to be reduced in bulk and processed at least to the stage where it can be both stored and transported without deterioration. This means that the plantation has to be equipped to carry out certain minimal factory or quasi-factory processes such as drying, curing, fermenting, distilling, grading, pressing and packing.

6. The growing of plantation crops is normally a labour-intensive undertaking, and the harvesting and processing of them is even more so. The labour supply is therefore a factor, in addition to conditions of soil and climate, that determines where plantation industries can be established. This heavy labour requirement frequently cannot be satisfied by what is available on the local labour market, which accounts for the historic connections, at various times, between the plantation industries and slave, indentured and immigrant labour. Since some at least of the labour will be required all the year round, and since some of it will have been brought from far away, the planter often finds himself responsible for the housing and welfare of large numbers of people.

7. Some plantation crops such as cotton and tobacco are annuals, but many are perennials that will not come into full bearing for several years. The labour requirements of even the annual crops make them expensive to grow, but in the case of the perennials, where there will be little or no return for several years, the capital investment required is considerable. Plantations are therefore capital-intensive enterprises, and as such are normally owned, these days, by companies rather than by individuals. With the growth of vertical organisation, many of them are owned by manufacturing companies concerned with assuring their supplies of raw materials. Firestone, Dunlop, Unilever and Tate & Lyle are all examples of manufacturers who are also plantation owners. One of the consequences of this is that, in the capitalist world, the plantations constitute almost the only agricultural sector in which the public can invest as shareholders.

8. Since planters generally have to sell their produce in distant markets to manufacturers and processors rather than to retailers and the consuming public, they are particularly dependent on the services of middlemen. Among these will be the agency houses who handle and bulk the crop at railhead or port, the shippers who trans-

port it thousands of miles and the produce brokers who determine the market. Since it is such a capital-intensive industry, it will be dependent also on the stockbrokers who deal in its shares, the investors who buy them and the bankers who provide large parts of the seasonal and working capital required. Plantation farming differs, in this respect, from traditional farming, which is very largely family financed and sells its crops at the farm gate. Those crops may then pass through several hands before reaching the public, but the farmer has a less direct and necessary connection with the middlemen of the produce, stock and money markets than does the planter.

9. Plantation crops are enormously important in the modern world in spite of the fact that, unlike traditional food crops, they are produced to satisfy the secondary rather than the primary needs of mankind. Our ancestors, indeed, never realised that there was any need at all for any of them, and managed to lead short, brutish, but doubtless satisfying lives without such commodities as sugar, tea, tobacco, coffee, chocolate, quinine, cotton, rubber or margarine. We, however, could not do so, possibly because the plantations have made us more civilised. If one defines civilisation as the process of advancing man's material well-being, and if man's well-being consists of discovering new needs and satisfying them, then the plantations must rank as civilising factors of the utmost importance. Nutritionalists and puritans alike may deplore our fondness for sugar and our dependence on such stimulants as tobacco, tea and coffee, but few of them would deny that these things have, in spite of all the propaganda against them, become almost as essential to civilised man as bread. Certainly we have learnt, from the occasional interruptions that occur in the supply of such things, that whenever they become scarce enough to become luxuries once more, something resembling a true food hunger, with all its political and social implications, results.

The plantations developed, of course, around certain plants – annuals, shrubs or trees – whose produce was either completely or comparatively unknown in Europe. Once the colonists had introduced that produce to Europe and made it available to the masses, Europeans acquired new needs. Many of these plants had been domesticated by the natives long before the colonists arrived, and were grown by them in gardens and plots for domestic use and even, to a limited extent, for trade. What the planters did in such cases was to systematise and greatly extend the cultivation of such plants. As a consequence, commodities that had either been unavailable to Europeans or available only to the richest of them quickly developed into popular necessities. One only has to remember how rapidly former luxuries such as sugar, cotton, tea and coffee became working-class necessities to realise what a transformation the plantations brought to life in Europe as well as in the colonies.

In some cases – and rubber is probably the most important of them – the plant had not even been domesticated by the time the colonists arrived, although the natives may have been harvesting it wild in the jungles and forests for centuries. In such cases, the planter had to start by domesticating the plant before he could decide how and where to grow it and what use to make of its produce. In these activities, he got most help from the botanists who, as plant hunters, plant breeders, practical gardeners and analytical chemists, were the indispensible all-purpose scientists of the eighteenth and nineteenth centuries. The botanists, more than anyone else, helped to break the Chinese quasi-monopoly of tea and the Brazilian monopoly of rubber.

10. The plantations did far more than merely change consumption patterns in Europe: they changed industrial patterns as well. New industrial districts, towns, even regions appeared to process such plantation crops as cotton, jute, sugar, tobacco and rubber. Great business houses grew out of the need to centralise the processes of bulking, grading, blending and packing coffee and tea. Many of London's financial institutions developed from the requirements of the plantation industries, which needed bankers, agents, brokers and shippers to provide the essential services that would finally bring their produce on to British and world markets. Many of our present distributive and retail organisations grew up to bring plantation produce to the consumer. The German language formally acknowledges the historic connections between the colonies and any grocer's shop, though it is doubtful whether the German consumer is any more conscious of them than the British. It is probably difficult for any European consumer to realise how heavily dependent he is on the plantation industries. Yet, from his first cigarette and early-morning cup of tea to his final return home

on some form of pneumatic tyred transport, the plantations continue to sustain, stimulate and support him.

11. Large profits have been made, and perhaps are still made, in the plantation industries, though more often by the agencies, brokers and industrialists than by the planters themselves. Large losses can also be made, though in this case the first sufferers are always the planters. Planters are, indeed, vulnerable in many ways. As agriculturalists they are even more exposed to the traditional dangers of farming than those who engage in mixed farming. Where only one crop is grown, frost, flood, storm, drought or disease can bring complete destruction, often not only of that year's crop but of a plantation which may have taken decades to establish. It has to be remembered, moreover, that the mere existence of an area of monoculture almost automatically increases the risk of plant disease and the amount of damage it causes.

Plantations tend to be grouped together in certain more or less circumscribed areas particularly suitable for the crop in question. Such areas may or may not be replicated in other parts of the world, but the mere proximity of the plantations to each other in any one region necessarily means that all of them will be more or less similarly affected by that season's growing conditions. The risks of a good harvest as well as of a bad one will not be spread as widely as with general farming, and it has to be remembered that the risk which attends a good harvest is glut just as the one that attends a bad one is famine.

Both glut and famine affect the markets for plantation commodities even as they do for any other agricultural produce. For plantation crops, however, supply and price fluctuations have a tendency to produce results that differ somewhat from the results produced by similar fluctuations in the staple agricultural crops. Demand for all agricultural produce tends to be inelastic. If a glut produces a sharp fall in price to the consumer, the increase in consumption that results will seldom compensate for the loss of income to the grower. This inelasticity is especially marked with plantation crops, most of which provide raw materials for industries. The demand for motor cars will not noticeably increase because the rubber for their tyres has suddenly become cheaper. The same is largely true of the plantation consumer products. Tea drinkers will not buy more tea merely because a pound of tea costs less in the shops than it did before. Precisely opposite considerations operate, however, in times of shortage. The plantation crops, as has already been said, are secondary commodities for which alternatives or substitutes can usually be found whenever prices rise too sharply. Tea drinkers can turn to coffee and coffee drinkers to tea, and both can, when obliged, reduce consumption when either commodity is dear. What is even more important is that, for most of the industrial crops, chemists have been able to synthesise analogues that will partially or completely replace the natural product whenever it becomes economic to do so. Man-made fibres, for example, are now able, for most purposes and at most price levels, to replace natural fibres, just as synthetic rubber is able, in part at least, to replace natural rubber whenever the latter becomes more costly. Moreover, once the industrial consumer has equipped himself to make use of the synthetic product, it will take very definite long-term economic advantages to induce him to return to the natural product.

Since most of the synthetics are produced by the petrochemical industries, the recent rise in the price of oil has begun to act in favour of the natural product. There can be little doubt that the plantation industries, with their infinitely renewable resources, will in the long run enjoy an increasing advantage over the synthetics produced from our finite stocks of hydrocarbons. Industrialists, however, generally operate in the short rather than in the long term, and the plantation industries cannot, however much they may wish it, allow their products to rise in price as sharply as oil costs have risen.

A completely free market for agricultural products has probably never existed, except for the one short period of less than a century when in free trade prevailed in Britain. Most governments are at least protectionist, and many are interventionist when it comes to matters of agriculture. In spite of this, the markets for agricultural produce are notoriously cyclical, and attempts by politicians to produce some sort of stability on national and international levels have met little success. No system yet devised of levies, quotas, deficiency payments, buffer stocks, consumer subsidies or supply management has made much difference to the fact that the producer seldom achieves that parity of income which he aspires to and the consumer seldom enjoys the price stability which he believes to be his right. This is a matter of considerable political importance to the plantation countries, which are, for the most part, located in what is now called the underdeveloped world. That is, they are the south part of the north-south dialogue which nowadays represents such an important element in international affairs. Most of these countries are, by comparison with the industrialised ones of the northern hemisphere, impoverished, and many of them depend heavily on the export to the industrialised nations of plantation products. For some of them, such products may constitute the largest part of their total export trade. Almost all the countries producing plantation crops therefore seek to establish larger, freer, higher priced and more stable markets for those crops, and their arguments in favour of this virtually monopolise whatever meaningful dialogue the two halves of the world currently engage in. Their model and inspiration is perhaps the very successful stranglehold over the industrialised countries established by the OPEC cartel. For several fairly obvious reasons, however, it is considerably more difficult to establish a cartel and a monopoly in rubber or tea than it is in oil. Even so, the concept of such a monopoly has always been attractive. The first plantation crops were, in fact, largely conducted as monopolies by the governments controlling them. Tea, rubber, silk, opium, even rhubarb were all, at one time, at least quasi-monopolies jealously guarded by the governments involved. Many of the early colonial wars had their origins in attempts to maintain or break such monopolies. For this reason the plantation crops have always been politically sensitive ones on the international level, though the possibility of monopolies has decreased with the wider spread of most plantation areas and the discovery of analogues and substitutes.

12. Plantation crops are also politically sensitive on the national level. Most plantation enterprises must, by their very nature, be capitalist enterprises. This is true even when it is state capitalism rather than private capitalism that is involved. Many of them are carried on in parts of the world where private capitalism is associated with a rejected colonialist past. This rejection is intensified when, as is so often the case, the capital invested is largely or entirely foreign, the management expatriate, the produce exported, with little value added to it locally for manufacture abroad, the price set in a foreign and not a domestic market, and the profits of production, as much as possible, repatriated to the country where

the capital originated. None of these are politically popular activities in any country. Even in the 'developed' countries, where foreign investment is generally welcomed, the conditions under which foreign capitalists prefer to invest are not. In most of the newly independent countries, where an almost obsessive suspicion of 'neo-colonialism' is common, both the desire for foreign investment and the resentment of it are intensified. Investment by foreigners in land is nearly always resented, since few countries are untouched by land hunger. When ownership of that land brings with it control over a staple export and over large bodies of native labour, the rational as well as the irrational occasions for resentment increase.

There are political risks, therefore, that attach particularly to the plantation industries, even when they are owned and managed by nationals. When they are owned and managed by foreigners, those risks intensify. The plantation industries are accordingly exposed to the dangers of having special and onerous taxes levied on their exports and profits, of having restrictions imposed on any repatriation of these profits, of having capital locked in, of being subjected to increasing pressures to ensure that a growing proportion of the ownership and management passes into local hands, while, at the end of it all, lie the final solutions of nationalisation and even expropriation. Yet, in spite of all these hazards – agricultural, economic and political – that attach to the plantations, they have always attracted and continue to attract British capital, British entrepreneurs and British managers. Why, one may ask, should this be so?

Some possible answers have already been suggested. Among them is the strong colonising instinct of the British which has not yet been stifled and which flows as much from an instinctive feeling for the land and for pioneering as from a desire to trade and grow rich. Landlessness may no longer be the compelling force it once was, even though there is more landlessness in Britain today than in most other civilised countries, but there is still, among many, a resentment of the urbanised, industrialised society we have created which denies access to the land to such a vast majority of people. These are all what might be described as psychological reasons, and must therefore be suspect, since any writer could imagine or invent them. There are two rather more solid reasons that have always attracted the British to the plantations. The first is that, in the tropical and sub-tropical countries where most of them are to be found, agricultural land has always been thickly settled and intensively worked by the indigenous population. There were no large empty areas of potentially arable land to be occupied by the new settlers, as there were in North America and Australasia. If they wanted land, they had to carve it out of jungles and mountain forests where normal agriculture would generally be difficult but where the plantation crops might flourish. The second and more powerful reason is the gamble inherent in plantation farming. All farming is, to a certain extent, a gamble, but the odds are greater, the chances of profit or loss increased, when plantation crops are attempted.

It may seem odd to talk of the merchant adventurer instinct in Britain today, where we seem to have settled for safety, uniformity and mediocrity under a series of nannying governments, yet that instinct survives, even though it can now only find its expression abroad. As we have already remarked, great fortunes have been made, and occasionally can still be made, in the plantations as well as great losses. Plantation booms such as the early tea and rubber booms could produce much the same result as a gold strike, and the British, as well as the Spaniards, have always been attracted by legends of El Dorado. It is this hope of profits far greater than any that can be made from more humdrum forms of farming that has always attracted men who would not otherwise have been attracted to agriculture, and induced entrepreneurs and investors who would have recoiled from the mere idea of putting their money into other forms of farming to put their money into plantation industries.

The East Indian or West Indian nabob, who had made his fortune in the plantations and had returned to buy his estate in the Shires and his seat in Parliament, was a common figure in nineteenth-century literature. Such different writers as Thackeray, Surtees and Peacock had satirised them. They were, together with the newly emerging cotton and railway magnates, the essential upstarts, and they shared with them the odium and the envy that attach to those who succeed in thrusting their way into what is supposed to be a closed and hieratic ruling class. In fact, such a class had disappeared with the Plantagenets. Ever since then, the British ruling classes have been fluid and easily penetrated. They have, as a consequence, been able to renew and strengthen themselves from generation to generation through successive infusions of thrusters whose only ticket of admission has been worldly success in some form or other, even in planting.

The plantations, in short, just as much as the Australian gold mines or the South African diamond mines, offered the adventurous a chance, however slender, of rapid enrichment and equally rapid social advancement. However slender that chance was, the thousands who failed, who spent their working lives on the plantations and either died there of malaria, cholera or drink, or else ended up in the genteel anonymity of Tunbridge Wells, Cheltenham or Peebles on a barely adequate pension, could still console themselves with the thought that, though they themselves might have worked hard for little ultimate reward, there were still one or two of them who had contrived to shake the golden mohur tree to greater effect.

This has been a chapter of introductory generalisations, none of them incontrovertible, some of them perhaps irrelevant. It has touched on the subjects of the colonies and the plantation industries in the most general way. The next chapter will be more specific, and will deal with one former colony and the plantation industries associated with it. Ceylon was where the Money and Boustead families first started in the plantation and agency businesses, and Ceylon therefore becomes the focus of our attention.

CHAPTER TWO

The Spicy Breezes

What though the spicy breezes
Blow soft o'er Ceylon's isle.
– Bishop Heber: Hymn

WHEN Ceylon was acquired as a colony by the British, it was acquired in a manner that has already been mentioned: that is, it was acquired inadvertently. To be more precise, it became part of the British Empire as a consequence of the vagaries of war and a certain amount of unexpectedly Machiavellian intrigue by a political amateur, Professor Hugh Cleghorn. Cleghorn was neither a Rhodes nor a Raffles. He was not even a Lawrence of Arabia, though his interest in Arab slave boys would seem to indicate a certain affinity. Yet, unprofessional though he was when it came to playing the Great Game, he can still claim to have added Ceylon to the Empire without shedding a drop of British blood and at a cost in monetary terms that was substantially less than the price of a single rotten borough.

One should, however, begin at the beginning. Ceylon was a much conquered and colonised island before the British acquired it. The aboriginal Yakkhos, early historians tell us, had been over-run, at various times, by Indian invaders from both the Gangetic and Coromandel coasts, and had been forced back into the jungles where such of them as survived did so in isolation as secretive and primitive hunters and food gatherers. Later came successive invasions by the 'Moors' (which meant no more than Moslems from any of the Islamic kingdoms to the West), the Portuguese and the Dutch. When the British suddenly and unexpectedly found themselves invading Ceylon, they were therefore doing no more than follow an established tradition.

There were at least two reasons why the island should invite invasions on this repetitious pattern. Its strategic position at the tip of the Indian sub-continent made it a useful staging and trading post on the route to the East Indies and China, as well as a potential naval station from which the entrances to the Bay of Bengal and the Arabian Sea might be controlled. In addition, however, Ceylon was always a sufficiently rich and fertile country to be attractive to any coloniser. Although the centre of the island is mountainous and thickly forested, the flat coastal plains are fertile and benefit from both the south-west and the north-east monsoons, the benefits of the latter being prolonged by the immense network of tanks and canals built on the east coast by ancient rulers. The plains have always, as a consequence, been thickly settled and intensively cultivated. Much of the celebrated wealth of the island, on the other hand, was drawn from non-agricultural sources, even though Ceylon was, for a long time, an important exporter of rice. There were the famous pearl fisheries, gems, gold, silver and ivory as well as jungle products such as sandalwood and camphor. But it was primarily as a spice island that it was valued and coveted. For nearly a century and a half, under the Dutch, it produced the whole of the world's crop of cinnamon.

Spices may not seem as important now as they were in the days before canning and freezing, and cinnamon may seem one of the less important of the spices. Nevertheless the world's consumption of it remained steady at around 400,000 lb. per annum, and the Dutch ensured that Ceylon's exports of the commodity remained stable at precisely that figure. They were, in this respect perhaps, the only power to succeed in matching world production to world consumption on a long-term basis. In spite of the United States' set asides and land banks, the European Community's Common Agricultural Policy, the FAO's buffer stocks and commodity agreements and the Soviet Union's Conquest of Nature and Virgin Lands policies, no other country, before or since, has succeeded in doing as much. It is true that the Dutch had to maintain a somewhat tight discipline over the producers and merchants in order to make a success of their policy, for they hanged anyone who ignored it. In this respect at least they had always been among the more robust of colonisers.

Cinnamon could not, at least until 1769, be considered a plantation crop since it was harvested by native bark strippers from wild trees growing in the jungle. The Dutch, unlike the British in later days, never succeeded in conquering the ancient kingdom of Kandy, the mountainous central region of the island where most of the forests and most of the wild cinnamon were to be found. When, in the middle of the eighteenth century, the then king of Kandy began to claim jurisdiction over all bark strippers working in his forests, the Dutch felt that their control over the crop might be threatened. They therefore decided to turn it into a plantation crop that could be grown entirely on land under their sole control. A large government cinnamon plantation was accordingly established at Mardana, and the farmers around Colombo were encouraged to start cinnamon gardens. In this way the crop was largely domesticated and kept even more completely under control. Cinnamon remained a Dutch monopoly for as long as the Dutch governed the island. One begins to understand how the Dutch East India Company was able, throughout the two centuries of its existence, to pay an average annual dividend of 18 per cent.

The cinnamon story needs, perhaps, to be rounded off, both because it demonstrates the difficulties of maintaining any plantation monopoly and because it leads us, eventually, to tea, and through tea to the Moneys. The Dutch had succeeded in maintaining their monopoly by establishing strict controls over the quality as well as the quantity of exports. They allowed only the finest bark to be shipped, and this denied the market to shippers from other countries where an equal quality control was not maintained and whose coarser grades of cinnamon were unable to compete with the fine qualities that came from Ceylon. The British, when they took over the government of the island, were unwilling or unable to maintain such strict controls. The quality of the exported cinnamon fell, and, as a consequence, other countries became able to compete with their coarser grades of bark. Finally, the bark of the much more widely spread cassia tree was found to be capable of competing with cinnamon bark of the qualities that were now exported once the strict Dutch controls had been removed. As a consequence of this, the European planters in Ceylon abandoned cinnamon as a crop and the native growers stopped grading altogether and sold only in bulk to compete with the coarse cinnamons from Java and the Indian and Chinese cassias.

This narrative, however, has not as yet got the British into Ceylon and the Dutch out of it, and the story of how that was done

is not without interest. There had always been a certain am-
bivalence in Anglo-Dutch relations, for the two countries had ever
since the days of the Stuarts struggled with each other for naval,
trading and colonial supremacy. That struggle had caused two
naval wars in Europe and several small campaigns in various parts
of the colonial world in the course of which efforts had been made
to eliminate each other's trade, traders and settlements. Yet the
long-term realities in Europe, as opposed to the colonies, obliged
the two countries to be allies rather more frequently than it obliged
them to go to war with one another. There had always been
religious, political and dynastic bonds between the two countries
that could never be completely forgotten in the heat of these commercial rivalries. What was far more compelling, however, was the
ever-present threat of French imperialism, which menaced not
merely the Netherlands but all of Western Europe.

The French Revolution added the threat of French Jacobinism
to that of French imperialism. When the French armies overran the
Netherlands, not without assistance from Dutch and Flemish
Jacobins, the Dutch reigning family took refuge in England, and
the restoration of the House of Orange became one of Britain's war
aims. This made the problem of the Dutch colonies a critical one.
None of them had, as yet, abandoned their allegiance and sided
with the French, but French agents were active in all of them, and
the possibility that French troops might be sent to reinforce and
control their garrisons could not be ignored. If the British moved in
before the French, they risked weakening the loyalist position and
driving the colonial Dutch into the arms of the French. If they did
not move before the French, they risked French troops returning in
force to areas from which they had comparatively recently been
ejected. The British position in India, especially, would be
threatened.

It was finally decided that the danger of acting was less than the
danger of doing nothing. Dutch colonies at the Cape and in the
East and West Indies were occupied by British troops, generally
with little or no resistance from the Dutch. The position in Ceylon
was a particularly delicate one. The Dutch garrison there was still
nominally loyal, but French agents were at work and no one knew
for how long that loyalty would be maintained or what resistance
might be offered to British troops moving into Ceylon from the
mainland.

It was at this stage that Professor Cleghorn intervened, and by intervening demonstrated what a haphazard affair the acquisition of a colony can sometimes be. The professor, in addition to holding the Chair of Civil History at the University of St Andrews, travelled a great deal on the Continent, where he may even have engaged in a certain amount of secret service work, as was the amiable habit in those unspecialised and amateur days. He certainly knew and was known to Dundas, first Viscount Melville, who was, before his fall from power, both uncrowned king of Scotland and Pitt's Secretary of State for War. He also knew, and this was equally important, a certain Swiss nobleman, the Conte de Meuron, who owned, among other things, a regiment of Swiss mercenaries which he hired out under the command of his brother. That regiment formed an important part of the Dutch garrison in Ceylon, which was not, in fact, particularly Dutch but was made up of locally recruited 'Malays' stiffened with Swiss and German mercenaries.

Cleghorn told Dundas that he believed he could induce the Conte de Meuron to travel out with him to Ceylon and there persuade his regiment to abandon the Dutch and join the British as soon as they landed. Dundas thereupon offered to pay for their journey and to give de Meuron £4,000 immediately and £6,000 a year for his regiment once it had entered British service. This prompt but hardly munificent offer started the two companions on a leisurely and comically varied journey that lasted seven months and took them from Venice to Alexandria and then down the Red Sea via Jiddah and Mocha to India. The voyage down the Red Sea was made in a ship captained by a Moor who insisted on pressing four of his concubines on the professor. The mate was a drunken Englishman, the gunner a black Christian called Paul and the man of all works a Chinaman. The helmsman constantly fell asleep, and Cleghorn discovered that de Meuron could not swim.

They had, however, their diversions, for there were on board

a number of very fine slave boys . . . who . . . by means of sweetmeats . . . have become very playful and familiar . . . also some eunuchs whom the captain purchased at Mocha, one of whom is the genteelest looking boy I ever saw . . . He has already contracted that look of diffidence and melancholy which distinguishes this order of being. I am told that he is an Abyssinian

and costs 300 dollars ... Our captain informs us that nine
out of ten who undergo this operation do not survive it ... The
little slaves are remarkably gay and lively and form a striking
contrast in this respect with the eunuchs of their own age, with
whom they rarely associate in any amusement. These boys are all
from eight to ten years of age; we have about a dozen in all and
one of them has become so great a favourite that I am resolved to
purchase him if I can get a Mohametan [*sic*] to purchase him in
his name and transfer him to me. He may cost me £10 or £15.

The professor, fortunately perhaps, failed in this venture since
the boy was destined for a Mohammedan priest in Bengal and so
was bespoken. He observed, however, that, in spite of the concubines and the slave boys, what the Arabs really loved most was
horses. He was taken to a stable in Mocha where everything was in
the most beautiful order and where, 'if by accident, an animal feels
a call in the middle of the night, its need is made known by a noise,
and the keeper brings in a "pot de chambre" for the purpose'. It
was at Mocha that the professor failed to join the convoy of Company ships, on one of which he proposed to make the rest of the
journey. They sailed out of harbour without him, in spite of the
fact that he had rigged up a Union Jack made of blue mosquito
curtain and red handkerchiefs. He was therefore obliged to make
the rest of the way to India in the company of the Moorish captain,
the Chinaman, the slave boys, the concubines and the somnolent
helmsman. When he finally landed in India, at Alenjo, he
discovered that the occupation of Ceylon had already begun and
that the British troops, under General Stuart had landed at the
north-eastern port of Trincomalee. Undismayed, Cleghorn and de
Meuron made a leisurely overland journey to the tip of the Indian
peninsula and finally joined General Stuart in Trincomalee almost
a year after leaving Venice.

There had, as far as one can gather, been no opposition to the
British landing at Trincomalee, perhaps because the Dutch garrison was stationed on the opposite side of the island around
Colombo. Since the members of that garrison were still nominally
loyal, it had been difficult for General Stuart to discover an actual
casus belli, and the two small armies were accordingly stuck *in situ*
looking at each other across the width of the island. There was
therefore still scope for Cleghorn and some role for de Meuron.

The first need was to communicate with the younger de Meuron in Colombo. Communication with that city had not entirely ceased with the British invasion. A trading boat was setting out with a load of wine and cheese for the garrison there. Cleghorn, maintaining a seemly secrecy, hid his message inside a cheese and persuaded the ship's captain to deliver it to de Meuron *frère*. It arrived at its destination and, after a certain amount of haggling over the price, the younger de Meuron led his regiment out to join the British as soon as they managed to move round the island and draw up in front of Colombo. The loss of nine hundred men and their addition to the strength of the forces confronting him represented a sufficient change in the balance of power to induce the Dutch governor to surrender without any show of resistance. Ceylon became a British possession and remained one until, after the Second World War, Britain decided to stop being an empire, without perhaps realising that for lack of an Empire she would become merely an overcrowded island living on memories of industrial and political supremacy that would fail to keep any Briton in the manner to which he believed himself entitled.

The Régiment de Meuron went on to serve in the British Army throughout the Napoleonic Wars, and was, in fact, only disbanded in 1816. The Conte de Meuron presumably drew £6,000 a year for it until he died or his force was disbanded. The professor, according to his diary, spent some time touring Ceylon, wrote a book on its pearl fisheries, and put some energy into criticising its former Dutch governors for their cruelty and rapacity. When he returned to Scotland he was given an honorarium of £5,000 by the government, with which he bought a property near St Andrews which his descendants still own. He was to be sent out to Ceylon, however, once more, this time as Chief Secretary. In that capacity he was imprudent enough to quarrel with the governor, the later Earl of Guildford, over a report sent to Whitehall about conditions on the island. He was, as a result, sent home again, to end his days in St Andrews, where, in a suitably Scottish apotheosis, he became Captain of the Royal and Ancient. He had anticipated, by almost two centuries, the modern type of academic who moves so easily between Academia and Whitehall or the Pentagon and who staffs, to no apparent advantage to anyone, the 'think tanks' which modern politicians rely on. Cleghorn had at least produced something definite in the shape of Ceylon, and he seemed to have been well aware of the dichotomy between thought and action that still distresses so many dons, for he wrote in his diary:

Learned retirement and secluded leisure for study is nonsense. The world is a school of letters as well as of business ... My ardent desire to visit foreign countries has been gratified to the utmost. I was a near observer ... of all the great events passing in France, and to a certain extent I became acquainted with all the great men of my time.

The inscription on his tombstone says of him that he was: 'The agent by whose instrumentality the Island of Ceylon was annexed to the British Empire.' As Doctor Johnson once remarked, 'In lapidary inscription a man is not upon oath.' Nor, indeed, is he able to mention everything that is of importance or interest in the life being recorded in stone. What this particular inscription omitted to mention was the fact that Cleghorn's career marked the beginnings of Ceylon's connections with a long line of British eccentrics.

Coffee, Tea and Europe

'The history of Ceylon,' someone once wrote, 'is the history of its crops.' If that be true, then what one has to call 'the cinnamon period' of Ceylon's history was drawing to its close, for reasons already been outlined, by about 1845. What one has to consider for the following three decades is the 'coffee period' of that island's history.

The great Ceylon coffee boom of this period had its origins even more in Europe than in Ceylon. It was not that the few Europeans then owning plantations in Ceylon suddenly turned to coffee and tea planting and then had to persuade the Europeans to accept these commodities, hitherto only used by the wealthy, in ever-increasing quantities. It was rather that an almost revolutionary change occurred in the European diet, and that this had created an increased demand for those products that Ceylon was in a position, at times, to satisfy.

If we ask what it was that brought about this change we have to fall back, in the first instance, on that universal explanation for almost all changes in nineteenth-century Europe: the Industrial Revolution. By urbanising a rapidly growing number of Europeans, the Industrial Revolution very considerably revolutionised their diets. Peasants in many countries were being turned into the industrial proletariat which was to be at once the principal characteristic and the principal problem of Western Europe for at least the next century. One of the consequences of being a member of the proletariat is that one has to eat and drink differently from peasants.

Peasants in any country are notably conservative in their diets. They live in a largely self-sufficient world and are accustomed to eating and drinking what they can produce themselves, or, failing that, what the neighbourhood produces. But once they have been proletarianised, once they have been denied any further access to the land, once they have become solely wage-earners and can no longer expect to be in any way food growers, their diet has to change, if only because it has to be drawn from different and more varied sources. As consumers they find themselves at the end of a long and complicated chain of supply instead of being no further away from their day-to-day food supplies than the distance that separates them from their gardens, their fields and their grazings.

It is important to remember that, for most peasants, those gardens and fields produced drink as well as food. Indeed, drink, whether it was milk, beer, wine or cider, was food. So long as a peasant could afford to drink something more than water – and in England, up to the middle of the eighteenth century, this was generally the case – what he drank contributed significantly to his nutrition.

It also, of course, added a certain amount of stimulus and pleasure to his otherwise laborious and even brutish life. For in early eighteenth-century England even a cottager expected to be able to brew and drink his own beer: small ale for everyday use and double brewed for special occasions. That drink, taken in fair quantity, represented an important part of his total calorie and vitamin intake. If he held no land and so could not grow and malt his own barley, he could still, until the taxes to pay for the French wars were imposed, expect to buy malt and hops locally at prices he could afford even on a day labourer's wage. His wife, unless he had been imprudent in marriage, would possess the skills and the rudimentary equipment with which to turn those products into his weekly supply of beer. Over and above this he could still, if he had rights of common, expect to keep a cow. Even if he had lost those rights he could, with a little ingenuity, as Cobbett pointed out, keep a cow or a couple of goats on the products and by-products of his garden.

In his diet, therefore, drink amounted to food he could afford. Indeed, what he could not afford, given the level of the rest of his diet, was for beer and milk to become luxuries he was forced to buy by the pint. Cobbett himself was an ostentatiously abstemious man who customarily drank nothing but twice-watered milk and invariably inveighed against drunkenness. Nevertheless he probably knew more about the lives and diet of the rural poor than any of his contemporaries. He always insisted that half a gallon of small ale a day was an essential part of the farmworker's diet. He was, however, a backward-looking man, radical though he was, and largely ignored the fact that his beloved 'chopsticks' were rapidly being turned into mill hands and slum dwellers. It was little use, therefore, his pointing out, as he did in a famous chapter of his *Cottage Economy,* how much cheaper and more wholesome home-brewed was than anything the chemically minded brewers could produce. The fact was that the readers he wrote for no longer had access to cheap malt and hops. If they were still farm labourers, they had, as a consequence of enclosures, lost most of their former self-sufficiency at the same time as taxes had driven food prices up and the beginning of the long decline in the prosperity of British agriculture had driven farm wages down. If they were men who had been driven, because of these hardships, into the towns, then not only was it improbable that they would have the money to spare for malt and hops, but there would be little room in their tenements or back-to-backs for the mash tub and the beer barrel. Their wives, moreover, would in all probability have been turned from housewives into factory hands. They would have forgotten their former skills, and would have had little time, in any case, for baking and brewing. The period of their future dependence on the grocer, the baker, the dairy, the brewer and, eventually, the canner, the freezer and the supermarket had begun.

It was even less use for Cobbett to proceed from there to his famous attack on tea. He was no doubt accurate down to the last halfpenny when he costed the expenditure in time, money and firing involved in keeping a working family going as tea drinkers and then contrasted it with their altogether happier position if they were content to remain brewers and drinkers of beer. But, accurate or not, the argument had become irrelevant since, for the majority, the options were no longer open. Neither the farmworker nor the factory worker could any longer expect home-produced beer, wine or milk to contribute to his diet. All of these could, of course, be bought from brewers, vintners and dairies, but acquired in that way they were too expensive to form part of the bulk diet. A gap had appeared, not only in the diet, but also in the social life of the poor, that had to be filled if urban and rural poverty were to be made endurable. Coffee and tea coming out of the new plantations in Ceylon, India, South America and even, in the end, Africa succeeded to some extent in filling that gap. Both were stimulants. Both, being drunk hot, did something to keep hungry people warm. Both, because of the even quite small quantities of milk and sugar added to each cup, provided some degree of nourishment. Both moreover possessed the additional advantage of being able, through their astringent action, to ease some of the pangs of hunger. Both were habit-forming and, as a consequence, gave rise to new social customs that influenced the domestic, working and leisure habits of the people. Looking back at the European situation in the first half of the nineteenth century, we could almost say that if the colonies had not already existed, if tea and coffee had not already been known, if planters and plantations had not been available for their mass production, then all of these would have had to be invented, if only to ameliorate, however slightly, the economic, social and dietetic shocks of the Industrial Revolution.

Coffee and Coffee Planters in Ceylon

It is traditionally believed that the coffee tree was originally brought to Ceylon by the Arabs. It could certainly be found growing wild in the jungle areas when the Portuguese first arrived in 1505. It is said that it was originally used by the Sinhalese for its fragrant white flowers, which provided an acceptable substitute for the frangipani blossoms so generally used for temple decorations and personal garlands. Be that as it may, the Dutch discovered towards the end of their rule in Ceylon that the material, if not the spiritual reward, lay in the bean rather than the blossom, since the consumption of coffee was becoming a well-established habit in the more prosperous households of Europe. They encouraged the Sinhalese peasants to cultivate it as a crop, but did not, as with

27

cinnamon, finance the establishment of plantations or attempt to create a coffee monopoly.

Coffee was not, however, planted very extensively by the peasants. It was not, in fact, a smallholder's crop. It grew best on the mountain slopes in the centre of the island, and these were still for the most part covered with primary jungle. To clear them, plant them and wait for a crop was not a smallholder's task. At that stage in Ceylon's development, or idyllic lack of development, foreign capital, foreign entrepreneurs and foreign adventurers were still awaited before coffee could be developed as the plantation crop that Europe needed.

The British, unlike the Dutch, hastened to spread their rule to the interior of the island, overcoming whatever objections were raised by the king of Kandy in a series of short, sharp campaigns. They found, among other things, that in those forested uplands the coffee tree, even in its wild state, flourished and fruited more successfully than it did on the coast. As a consequence, it was little more than twenty years after the occupation of the island that the first attempts at establishing what could properly be called coffee plantations were made. The two initial planting were made on an estate at Gangarooa belonging to the island's governor, Sir Edward Barnes, and one at Sinnapitiya that belonged to the military commander of the Kandy district, Lieutenant-Colonel Bird. Part of this last estate passed, some time later, into the ownership of the Bousteads, who will remain, from now on, central characters in this book. They later lost it, however, to the Oriental Bank in the great coffee slump to which the bank itself fell finally victim.

What is worth noting at this stage is the fact that in Ceylon, unlike India, British officials, officers and civilians were rapidly able to acquire land. In India, all of the land had been in ownership of some sort or another, and most of it had been intensively cultivated for many centuries before the East India Company embarked on the lengthy administrative task of confirming and registering title to the vast acreage it had, almost unwittingly, acquired. In Ceylon, on the other hand, much of the newly conquered uplands consisted of jungle and forest, little of which had been cleared and even less cultivated. The new colonial government assumed, rightly or otherwise, that an absence of cultivation necessarily meant an absence of ownership and that all such areas became, as *bona vacantia*, Crown property. As such they could be retained or alienated as the Crown saw fit. It needs to be remembered that in those days Crown lands, in Britain as well as in the colonies, were thought of not as a trust, but as a convenient central fund out of which rewards, merited or otherwise, could be paid to the Crown's servants and opportunities for investment be offered to would-be colonists. These were not thought of, at the time, as corrupt practices. People served the Crown and, in the case of soldiers, bought their commissions in order to do so, not for what they would be paid by way of salary, but for what they might reasonably expect to acquire as the perquisites of service. In the same way, colonies could not be developed, and if they were not developed they would represent a drain on Britain's resources unless potential colonists could be induced to emigrate. The offer of cheap land, either freehold or on a long lease at peppercorn rent, was, given the land hunger of those days, the most powerful of all inducements.

The coffee boom now starting intensified the scramble for Crown lands in Ceylon. In 1834, a mere 337 acres were alienated, while by 1841 this figure had soared to 78,658. Much of this land was, of course, bought by speculators for resale at a profit, and so by no means all of it was planted. Nevertheless, the acreage actually under coffee grew from 4,000 in 1836 to 37,000 in 1845. Those who were already in Ceylon as officials, officers or mere civilians were perhaps the first to appreciate the possibilities and rush to acquire land. From the Governor down to a colonial chaplain, and including the Commander of the British Forces, Sir John Wilson, who will concern us later, almost everyone wanted to add coffee planting to whatever other occupation he was engaged in. People came out to Ceylon to invest in coffee land as they might have gone out, a few years later, to California to stake out a claim in the gold diggings. When the first coffee crisis came in 1847 as a consequence of the removal of protective duties in Britain which brought the price of coffee down from 100s. to 45s. a hundredweight, or less than the cost of production, one of the earliest historians of Ceylon, Sir Emmerson Tennant, remarked rather sourly that the land rush in Ceylon differed from other gold rushes only in the fact that while the goldminers worked hard to disinter gold, the coffee planters worked equally hard to bury theirs for good.

Though some of the early plantings were made on lowland where clearing and planting were relatively easy, it was soon realised that the forested slopes of the uplands, however difficult they might be to clear, provided the most favourable sites. Hundreds of thousands of acres of forest in the central mountains were felled and the timber burnt off to make way for coffee, which was planted among the charred and blackened stumps in any pocket of soil that would offer root-hold. Those who laboured in this way to clear the slopes were, without being aware of it, preparing the way for the tea planters, for when coffee finally failed in Ceylon because of disease, the only consolation the ruined planters could discover was that most of the upland sites they had chosen for their coffee were sites that were also particularly suitable for tea.

Nor was it only in this way that the coffee planters acted as trail-blazers for the tea planters. Although local labour could be and was employed for clearing and planting, the Sinhalese showed little or no desire to engage in routine plantation work. They would work hard on specific tasks, but they refused to think of themselves as permanent plantation hands and wage-earners. They were intelligent enough to prefer the communal life of the village to the tighter disciplines of the estate lines, and were lucky enough, in most cases, to get all they needed from subsistence farming, therefore seeing no need to work to European rhythms. This meant that labour had to be recruited from elsewhere. The Dutch had already begun to recruit Tamils from the poverty-stricken areas of southern India for work in the cinnamon gardens, and the British now began to recruit there for their coffee plantations. Even though the work was largely seasonal, instead of all the year round as it was to be with tea, labour recruited from the Malabar Coast increased rapidly from 4,000 workers in 1841 to 74,000 in 1844. Recruitment and the transport of labour were left, at first, to Tamil gang leaders and the recruits undoubtedly suffered great hardship before they finally reached the comparative prosperity and security of the estate lines. Eventually the newly formed Planters' Association of Ceylon established a committee to supervise and improve existing methods of recruitment and travel. Like so many other such committees, one of its first acts was to secure financial backing from the government for its philanthropic but not entirely disinterested projects.

Coffee pioneered the way for tea in Ceylon in other ways than by opening up the jungle and recruiting labour. It brought about the early development, in London as well as in Ceylon, of the elaborate infrastructure needed to support any large-scale plantation industry. In Ceylon, a start had to be made on improving the almost non-existent lines of communication that led from the interior to the ports. In Colombo itself, the necessary plant and port facilities were established. These alone made it possible for the new plantation products to arrive on the European market. That market was, primarily, in London, and the City had to establish, outside the existing organisation of the East India Company, the finance needed for the creation and running of the plantations as well as the marketing and distribution outlets for their produce. What was most important of all, perhaps, was the gradual appearance, back in Ceylon, of the new professionals, the men who were to be even more important to the tea industry than to the short-lived coffee industry. They were, of course, the men who managed the estates and the agency houses.

Plantation Owners and Plantation Managers

The first coffee plantations, as has been seen, were on the whole established and owned by men who were not themselves planters. If they were in Ceylon, they were already engaged in other occupations, and if they were in England, they necessarily had to leave the making and managing of the plantations to others. In both cases, they were investors rather than cultivators, and in this they were typical of the future course of the plantation economy, where ownership and actual management were nearly always to be separated.

There were, of course, some plantation owners who abandoned whatever they had been doing in either Ceylon or Britain in order to devote all their time to plantation work. These were, however, in the minority. Most owners found it necessary to engage managers, or superintendents as they came to be called, to run the plantations for them. As a corollary, many of them, particularly if they were corporate owners in Britain, had also to find men who would, as it were, manage the managers for them, overseeing their work, providing advice, supplies and local finance, attending to the shipment and even the sale of the produce, acting in the purchase and sale of land, recruiting new or extra managerial staff if that became necessary, and reporting back on what was happening to the absentee owners'. They combined, in short, the roles of estate agent, consultant, merchant and confidential man of affairs. They were the men of the agency houses who were of such great importance in the economics of the Middle and Far Eastern colonies.

Before discussing the agency houses, however, it is interesting to look briefly at contemporary accounts of the new breed of plantation manager. That such a man was needed is demonstrated by Sir Samuel Baker's description, in his book *Eight Years' Wandering in Ceylon,* of two plantation owners whom he met, some time in the 1850s, in the Galle Face Hotel in Colombo:

> I was soon engaged in conversation with them and one of my first questions naturally turned upon sport. 'Sport!' exclaimed the two gentlemen simultaneously, 'sport! There is no sport to be had in Ceylon!' 'At least the race week is the only sport I know of' said the taller gentleman . . . 'I have an estate in the interior and I have *never* seen a wild elephant.'

Since Baker was already on the way to becoming one of the most famous shikars of all time, his later fame as an explorer stemming principally from his travels in search of big game, and since he had come out to Ceylon nominally to farm, but in practice to kill boar, elk and wild elephant across the length and breadth of the island in very great numbers, he felt bound to explain that:

> I subsequently discovered that my new and non-sporting acquaintances were coffee planters of a class then known as the Galle Face planters, who passed their time cantering about the Colombo race-course and idling in the town, while their estates lay a hundred miles distant, uncared for and, naturally, ruining their proprietors.

Since Baker himself spent far more time hunting than he did attending to his farm, and since it was eventually left to his younger brother to turn it from a misconceived and faltering farming venture into a flourishing tea estate, the famous hunter's remarks about 'Galle Face planters' may perhaps be unjustified. One should, to be fair, balance against them the example of Archdeacon Glenie of Colombo. His particular cure of souls was worth £2,000 a year to him. Nevertheless he had to be ordered by the Secretary of State in 1841 to devote less of his time to planting coffee on his estates and more of it to his ecclesiastical duties. Within two years he had resigned as archdeacon and gone to Nuwara Eliya to devote the rest of his life to coffee. But then, as Baker amiably remarked: 'Coffee planting in Ceylon has passed through the various stages inseparable from every mania.'

For the most part, however, the men engaged in the undeniably arduous and lonely task of making and managing the coffee plantations were not pluralistic archdeacons but the new breed of professional superintendents. What sort of men were they? P. D. Millie, in his book *Thirty Years Ago* (Colombo, 1878), says, rather sweepingly, that few of them had any education and even fewer had any experience of agriculture. They were 'people who as adventurers came to the country or were bought out of the regimental ranks'. Yet, he adds, they all strangely ended up as captains. For, he says, 'Take the Ramboda district in 1854. With the exception of the estate above the bridge, they were all Captains from Kondegalla down to well into Pussellawa, and even there, also, the Captains flourished.'

Colonel Edward Money, who will be met in all his eccentric glory in the next chapter, and whose military title was undoubtedly genuine, it having been earned in both the Indian and Turkish armies, had something very similar to say about the early tea planters in Assam in the 1850s. In his celebrated *Prize Essay on the Cultivation and Manufacture of Tea in India*, he states that:

> I believe there is nothing will pay better than Tea if embarked on with the necessary knowledge . . . It was madness to expect aught but ruin under the conditions which the cultivation was entered on in the Tea-fever days. People who had failed in everything else were thought quite competent to make plantations. 'Tis true Tea was so entirely a new thing at that time [that] but few could be found who had any knowledge of it. Still, had managers with some practice in agriculture been chosen, the end would not have been so disastrous. But any one – literally any one – was taken, and tea planters in those days were a strange medley of retired or cashiered army and naval officers, medical men, engineers, veterinary surgeons, steamer captains, chemists, shop-keepers of all kinds, stable-keepers, used-up policemen, clerks, and goodness knows who besides!

There is again, perhaps, a certain lack of justification for such strictures. The colonel himself had failed as a tea planter in the early days, possibly because an army training and a brief encounter with estate work in Hungary were not necessarily the best preparations for a career in tea planting. Nevertheless, as a consequence of his essay, his inventions and his later business career, all of which revolved around tea, he ended up as an acknowledged expert. All of which tends to confirm the old saying, whose truth any honest author will subscribe to, that, 'Those who can, do, and those who can't write books about it.'

Whatever their background and their competence, those early superintendents had to live rough and work hard for what was, considering the returns the owners enjoyed, remarkably little reward. They would rarely be paid more than £200 a year and their board, and the last, according to contemporary accounts, was not worth very much. Here is how Capper, writing his book *Old Ceylon* in 1878, describes how one of the early superintendents was housed:

> This miserable little cabin could not have been more than twelve feet long by about six feet wide, and as high at the walls. This small space was lessened by heaps of tools . . . sundry boxes and baskets, an old rickety table, and one chair. At the farther end, if anything could be far in that hole, was a jungle bedstead formed by driving green stakes in the floor and walls and stretching rope across them. I could not help expressing astonishment at the miserable quarters provided for one who had so important a charge, and such costly outlay to make. My host, however, treated the matter very philosophically . . . indeed he told me that when he had finished putting up this little crib . . . and was seated, cigar in mouth, inside the still damp mud walls, he thought himself the happiest of mortals.

His working dress, as reported by Capper, would consist of:

> A sort of wicker helmet . . . covered with a long padded white cloth which hung down his back like a baby's quilt. A shooting jacket and trousers of checked country cloth, immense leech gaiters fitting close inside the roomy canvas boots, and a Chinese paper umbrella made up his singular attire.

His amusements, in those early days of isolated living, were few, and consisted principally, if we can trust contemporary accounts, of drinking. Interminable crates of beer would be carried up-country to satisfy his quotidian requirements, and these ensured that almost every planter's shanty was distinguished, sooner or later, by a pyramid of empty bottles outside its door. It must be remembered, however, that sweat came easily in that climate and that bodily liquids needed to be replaced more frequently than in the conventicles and tabernacles of the total abstainers. It was on his rare visits to town, however, accompanied by some, perhaps, of his scattered neighbours, that drinking for pleasure, as opposed to necessity, really started. In a long poem, William Skeen, at that time a local poetaster, describes how:

> An efflorescence of wild mirth,
> Bursting restraint, gave sudden birth
> To strangest vagaries and vents,
> When, from their forest-life and tents
> Or rude thatch'd huts and ruder fare,
> To town they rush'd, and freely there,
> Like sailors fresh from year long cruise
> All cock-a-hoop for aught to amuse;
> Or Californian diggers, wild
> To squander gold, dust, nuggets piled,
> Gave to their spirits high the rein
> And heedless thus, while in the vein,
> O'erflowing with convivial glee,
> And rash in their rare jollity,
> Grave Mrs Grundy, sober, prim,
> Outraged and shock'd and render'd grim!

It was not until the plantation industry had established itself as a serious and long-term enterprise that a second and different generation of superintendents began to appear. Many, if not most of these were Scots, recruited because they already had some experience of gardening, farming or estate work. They brought with them a background of experience in growing things, if only turnips or Scots pine or roses. Even more important, they brought with them their native habits of industry, frugality and thrift, and that understanding of commerce that has so seldom deserted the Scots and which has ensured that they should be, in so many ways, the Chinamen of Europe. They found, in the uplands of Ceylon, a Douanier Rousseau version of their native Highlands, and as a consequence adopted them as their natural home. One of the reasons for the Act of Union had, after all, been to allow Scotsmen access to the English colonies, since they could claim none of their own after the disasters of the Darien settlement. Dundas, in his period of power, had ensured that India should provide openings for any Scot who aspired to make his fortune there. But perhaps nowhere in all the Asian colonies was the Scottish influence more dominant than in Ceylon. Each Scot who settled there tended to send back to Scotland for more of his clan until one of them, Hugh Moir, was able to claim that there were no less than fourteen men from the small Scottish town of Laurencekirk settled around him in the Ceylon uplands. It is small wonder, then, that the names of the planters, and eventually of the plantations, read like extracts from some Scottish directory.

It was not, perhaps, until the turn of the century that plantation management began to attract younger sons of the gentry as much as it attracted the younger sons of small Scottish farmers. By that time, of course, some of the physical and social hardships, though not all the economic ones, had begun to disappear from plantation life in Ceylon, and a young man coming out as a 'creeper' or pupil could look forward to enjoying many of the advantages enjoyed by a country squire at home together with the additional freedoms traditionally attached to life in a colony. In the end, and towards the end of it all, planters in Ceylon were expected to be members of at least the middle class either by birth or adoption. Some time during the 1930s, A. P. Herbert, after visiting Ceylon, was able to explain in *Punch* that the better the public school the planter had been to the less he had to do to grow the best tea. For the present, however, we are still back in the pioneering days of the Ceylon plantations, and need to take a brief look at those other pioneers who started the agency houses.

The Agency Houses

In the hey-day of the East India Company it had been difficult for independent merchants to establish themselves in India. The company was always jealous of its trading monopolies. The Cape and Ceylon, however, were, as newly acquired Crown Colonies, more open to private traders, several of whom established themselves, from the earliest days, in their initial and primary roles as middlemen. They traded two ways, bringing in British goods for sale locally and buying local produce for export and sale in Britain. They found, almost inevitably, that they had to both give and take credit. They took credit from the British suppliers; they gave credit to their local customers and, in increasing degree, to the local planters who would eventually provide the produce they traded in. Since there was, in the early days, no banking system in Ceylon, they became, in effect, bankers, providing the short-term capital needed to carry a crop to harvest, or alternatively arranging for credit to be made available from England.

The consequences that flowed from their activities as bankers were, in the early days at least, as important as those that flowed from their activities as traders. Before giving credit, they would have to establish the credit-worthiness of their customers. Since many of these would be planters, it meant that they had to acquire some expertise in plantation matters. In cases where a customer defaulted, they had, if necessary, to be prepared to take over his plantation and run it. To avoid such a necessity, they had also to be in a position to give advice, both technical and financial, just as in establishing credit-worthiness they had to be able to survey and value the plantation which provided the security for the loan. To meet these requirements, they would normally co-opt or take into partnership an experienced planter who could provide the expert knowledge in such matters they might not possess. This provided the beginnings of the visiting agent system that was later to become such an important part of agency work. Since, however, the agents were primarily merchants and adventurers ready to turn their hands to any diversification so long as it was profitable, rather than true bankers interested only in lending, the expert knowledge they had to possess in planting matters often led them to turn to planting themselves whenever the opportunity to do so seemed suitable.

Their rapidly acquired expertise in plantation matters was valuable to others than themselves. It was soon established that they could sell their knowledge to absentee owners in Ceylon and Britain, both of whom would come to depend on them for the sort of supervision an estate agent would give a landowner in Britain. What was to become eventually even more important was the fact that when, in the end, they did retire to Britain, the knowledge they brought back with them, and the connections they had built up with bankers and brokers at home, would be of great value to the increasing number of people who wished to invest as shareholders in the new companies being formed to take advantage of first the coffee and then the tea booms. Out of this developed the custom for a colonial agency house establishing a counterpart in London, managed generally by a retired partner or partners. These, in their turn, played an increasing part in the floating of new plantation companies once the need for capital became more than a private plantation owner could supply.

Finally, as the plantation industries came to play an increasingly important role in Ceylon's economic life, so the agency houses moved into prominence. They brought new technologies and new amenities to the island. They started new industries. In the political field, they were the people who spoke to the governor on commercial and economic matters and who forced the pace whenever expansions to the economy or to the colony were considered. As leaders of the local civilian community, they would provide the people who were elected to the Council or the Assembly, who were made Justices of the Peace and who ran the charities and voluntary institutions so important in colonial life. Eventually they might develop into one of the great banking and trading houses such as Guthries or Jardine Mathiesons, or they might continue as a split Ceylon/London agency house or, in times of crisis, like their planter clients, they might be dragged down into bankruptcy. Whatever their eventual fate, they were empire builders who also acted as midwives and governesses to the plantation industries.

The Death of Coffee in Ceylon

Medical and other historians have frequently written books attempting to prove that bacteria, viruses and fungi have had more influence on man's history than have men themselves. Without wishing in any way to adopt such a determinist view of history, one has to admit that the Black Death, syphilis, measles and smallpox have had their historic influences. So, too, have the diseases of animals and plants. The history of Africa might have been different had it not been for the tsetse fly and the anopheles mosquito. The history of Ireland might have been different but for the potato blight. The history of Ceylon and of tea drinking in England and the whole history of Anglo-Chinese relations could have been different had it not been for the coffee rust, *Hemileia vastratix*.

Coffee rust is said to have spread to Ceylon from the Horn of Africa, the spores of the fungus being carried there on the southwest monsoon. The strains of *Coffea arabica* which were then grown in all that area were far more prone to attack and damage

Up-country Ceylon view, c. 1860.

than those of *C. robusta* which are now normally grown in coffee-producing areas. The fungus attacks the leaves which die, leaving the tree defoliated. This has its effect, of course, on berry production, and the effect is cumulative, for though leaves may appear the following year, the rust continues, and with it continues the diminution of the crop. The disease first appeared in Ceylon in 1869 on the Gallolla estate. Within five years every coffee-growing district in Ceylon had been infected. Within ten years the average yield per acre had declined from four and a half to two hundred-weights per acre. There was no cure or prevention. Copper sprays, the standard fungicides, were useless. The death of the Ceylon coffee industry took some time, largely because the planters were reluctant to believe that anything so permanent as the death of their industry could happen. They kept discovering remedies and symptoms of regeneration in their trees. The more pessimistic, however, began to look around for substitute crops. Some planted cinchona, whose bark provided the quinine that was, at that time, as valuable as gold. Within a few years the limited market for the product was glutted and the consequent fall in price made the cinchona plantations uneconomic if not completely valueless. The more experimental planters, however, began to look towards India, and in particular towards Assam, where attempts were being made to establish a tea industry that would finally break the Chinese monopoly in that commodity.

CHAPTER THREE

Tea and the Entry
of the Moneys

'Tea, although an Oriental,
Is a gentleman at least . . .'
– G. K. Chesterton: 'The Song of Right and Wrong'

THE Emperor Shen Nung, who reigned in China somewhere
around 2700 B.C., is traditionally credited with the discovery
of tea. Whether this is so or not, it is always of help to any historian
to have a starting date, however apocryphal. It is certainly true,
however, that the Chinese have been growing and drinking tea for
many thousands of years. But so, too, have the Shan people of
Burma and Siam. For the fact is that the tea plant – *Camellia
sinensis* – can be found growing wild over an area that stretches for
1,200 miles north and and south and 1,500 miles east and west,
from China down to Vietnam and from Nagaland to Thailand.
There are, of course, varietal differences to be seen over this wide
area. In the harsher climate of China, *Camellia sinesis* is a bush that,
even when unpruned, seldom grows to more than ten feet in height,
whereas in Assam it is a forest tree that can grow to well over thirty
feet in its wild state. Nevertheless, these closely related members of
the Camellia family will grow, and when domesticated produce tea,
anywhere inside this region where the soil is acid, the rainfall not
less than forty or fifty inches a year, and the variation between the
hot and cold seasons not too marked.

It was, however, undoubtedly the Chinese who first introduced
the habit of drinking and, occasionally, the practice of growing tea
to the world outside the tea belt. They brought it to Japan, it is
said, in the eighth century A.D., and although the Japanese quickly

41

learnt how to grow it, it took them five centuries to learn that it was a beverage. Until then they treated it as a medicine, which may seem less strange when one realises that even now, in China, the leaf is frequently pickled and eaten as a vegetable. Tea first reached Europe in any quantity at the beginning of the seventeenth century when the sea routes to China were opened. By the beginning of the eighteenth century, the Honourable East India Company had established a depot in Canton and was beginning to exercise that monopoly over the tea trade that it maintained for the next hundred years. The quantities exported from China increased rapidly. By 1805, England alone was importing more than seven million pounds of China tea a year. In 1880, the climacteric year for the China tea trade, over 300 million pounds were exported from China, of which well over half came to England. Tea, by that time, had become an established British institution, just as New Zealand lamb and the roast beef of old Argentine were to be twenty years later.

Before the middle of the nineteenth century, however, the supply position had already begun to change. In 1833, the East India Company lost its legal monopoly in China. The Chinese government had never approved of it, and the company itself was beginning to look round for alternative sources of supply which would be more immediately under its control, and which would not involve paying for the tea in silver, which caused a bullion crisis, or in opium, which caused a moral one.

In 1834, Lord William Bentinck, then Governor-General of India, took the historic step of appointing a committee to study the possibilities of growing tea in India. For a number of reasons, the remote and newly acquired province of Assam attracted that committee's attention. It was, in the first place, the part of India that was closest to the tea-growing areas of China. It was known that tea grew wild there in the jungles, and it was believed that these were the survivors from former tea plantations. Finally, Assam was a wild, unpopulated area that produced little or no revenue. If tea could be established there commercially, then planters, British as well as Indian, might be tempted to go there to open up the jungles and establish a new industry.

The committee was unanimous in its opinion that Assam was the area where tea ought to be grown. What it could not agree on was what sort of tea to grow. Wallich, the famous curator of the Botanic

Gardens at Calcutta, thought that seed ought to be brought from China in order to establish, on Indian soil, a counterpart of the Chinese tea industry. Others believed, equally firmly, that seed or seedlings from the tea that already grew wild in Assam ought to be used. In the event, both had their way and neither prevailed. Seed was actually brought back from China, grown on in the Botanic Gardens and then dispatched for field trials. Others, at the same time, experimented with seed and seedlings from the Assam jungles. The larger-leaved, deeper-rooted Assam varieties, even when domesticated and pruned to a bush, did better on their native soils than the imported Chinese varieties which only really flourished at high altitudes where something resembling the thinner soils and harsher climate of China were to be found. In fact, however, the difference between the varieties was largely blurred. They were phenotypes rather than genotypes, and centuries of hybridisation had ensured that no clear lines of genetic difference could be established.

Tea growing in Assam, once it started, was very different, however, from tea growing in China. In the latter country it had always been a smallholder's crop, with no more of it grown on any one holding than could be picked and cured by family labour. It was cured, for the most part, as green tea. That is, it was wilted for only a very short period, was not allowed to ferment, and was quickly heated in pans to destroy the enzymes and so kill the leaf. Thereafter it was rolled by hand, dried and packed. Treatment such as this suited the delicately flavoured and scented leaves of the Chinese tea plant. There was no harshness in them that had to be eliminated by wilting and fermenting. In the new tea industry of Assam, almost everything was different. The tea gardens, as they were called, were from the outset large-scale plantations covering hundreds of acres and needing the constant attention of a very large labour force. The quantities picked every day soon made it necessary to handle the crop on a factory rather than a cottage scale. Although some Chinese were brought in at the beginning to advise on what were then the mysteries of manufacturing tea, it was soon found that their methods were suited to neither the size nor the nature of the Assam crops. The mere size of a day's picking on any plantation meant that hand labour in the curing had to be abandoned just as soon as machines could be devised for rolling, drying and grading the leaf. The leaves themselves were not delicate enough to be turned into green tea. They had to be wilted and fermented and so turned into black tea in order to mellow the harshness and strength of the infusion.

Once the Assam planters had learnt how to grow and handle their crop, however, the resultant teas quickly found favour with the British public, who preferred the new, stronger Indian teas to the China ones they now condemned as commonplace. If they had not done so before, they now began to add milk and sugar to the cup to soften its potency. It was because of this that tea began to make some real contribution to the British diet. A cup of plain tea contributes about four calories and a small amount of vitamin B to the diet. When milk and sugar are added, this is increased to forty calories and a small amount of protein. Since the British drink six cups of tea a day on average, it can be seen that tea drinking began to contribute about 240 calories to the daily diet, and this could amount to 10 per cent of the total calorie intake of the poor.

The first London auction of Assam tea was in 1839. As soon as the public became accustomed to it, good prices were obtained, and this was the signal for the first and perhaps the wildest of all the tea booms to start. Individuals and companies rushed to put their money, and sometimes their labour, into tea plantations. As Colonel Money expressed it in his *Prize Essay* :

Individuals and Companies rushing into tea bought tracts of five, ten, fifteen and twenty thousand acres ... I conceive there was a hazy idea that if 500 acres paid well, 1,000 would pay double and that eventually even two or three thousand acres would be put under tea and make the fortunate possessor a *millionaire* ... Again, companies and proprietors of gardens ... gave their managers simple orders to extend, not judiciously, but in any case. What was the result? Gardens might be seen in those days with 200 acres of so-called cultivations but with 60 or even 70 per cent vacancies. Many managers at that time had no experience to guide them in the manufacture of tea; each made it in his own way, and often turned out most worthless stuff ... Indian tea was a new thing then; the supply was small, and it fetched a comparatively much higher price than it does now ... Often in those days was a small garden made of 30 or 40 acres, and sold to a Company for 150 or 200 acres! I am not joking. It was done over and over again. The price paid, moreover, was quite out of proportion to even the supposed area. Two or three lakhs of rupees (£20,000 or even £30,000) have often been paid for such gardens, when not more than two years old, and forty per cent of the existing area vacancies. The original cultivators 'retired', and the Company carried on. With such drags upon them . . . could success be even hoped for? Certainly not.

By 1886, India, in spite of all the colonel's strictures and the collapse of the first tea boom, was exporting as much tea as China to the British market. This breaking of China's monopoly did not, however, go unnoticed. Tea was being planted as early as the middle of the last century in Natal, Transcaucasia and Brazil, and in the island of Ceylon, where coffee was still king in spite of the first slump in 1847, a few people were already beginning to think about tea as an alternative. Once again, it all started with the botanists. In 1839, Dr Wallich, whom we have already met, sent some seed of the recently discovered Assam tea to Mr Normansell who was Superintendent of the Botanic Gardens at Peradeniya; and followed it up, one year later, with a consignment of plants. Some of these were sent by Normansell to a planter at Nuwara Eliya with directions for cultivating them. This was done after representations had been made to the government that tea was likely to be a new and profitable speculation which would give rise to a valuable source of revenue. In spite of this, nothing was done commercially with the plants at Peradeniya and Nuwara Eliya except to allow them to grow into trees. The only other effort made at that time to grow and even manufacture tea was made on the Pusellawa estate of the brothers Gabriel and Maurice Worms. It is a part of the splendid oddness of the Ceylon story that these two German Jews, who were both men of fortune, as befitted collaterals of the Rothschilds, should have abandoned high finance and high society in order to become large-scale and extremely successful coffee planters in Ceylon. The story, which has probably been embellished, has it that Maurice Worms brought some tea plants back from China and planted them out in a nursery at Pusellawa, which was one of their estates. He also brought back a Chinaman to look after them, even though only a very small planting was involved. Sufficient tea was eventually picked and cured, under the supervision of the Chinese expert, for the Worms to be able to send small gifts of tea to their friends in England. Unkind critics pointed out that the eventual cost of that tea must have been in the region of £5 a pound. Nevertheless it provides that the first record we have of tea actually being grown and cured in Ceylon and exported to England. It seems, when one looks at it, a suitable thing for a member of the House of Rothschild to have done.

By the early 1860s, the Planters' Association of Ceylon was beginning to worry about the over-production of coffee. They were still unaware, of course, of the fact that, in a very few years, *Hemileia vastratix* was going to solve the problem for them. They decided that tea and cinchona were suitable alternative crops. Encouraged by what had happened in India with tea, they sent an experienced planter, Arthur Morice, to Assam and the other developing tea districts to report on the suitability of the crop for Ceylon. On his return, he submitted an exhaustive and admirable report which recommended, among other things, that Ceylon was a suitable area, that seed and plants from Assam should be used, and that, in order to produce only high-quality teas suitable for the London market, upland rather than lowland tea should be grown.

The report was acted upon with remarkable swiftness. A parcel of seed was ordered from Assam and was given, on its arrival, to James Taylor, superintendent of the Loolecondera Estate, and a man who had already made a name for himself by his trial plantings of cinchona. He raised them to seedlings and planted them out, and by doing so earned himself the title of Father of Ceylon Tea. When, very few years afterwards, the blight destroyed the Ceylon coffee industry, causing many plantations to be abandoned and almost half the planters to leave the island, there remained the example of Taylor and a few other pioneers to point the way to a new crop and a new extension of the plantation industry.

The General

This has, hitherto, been a story of plants and plantations rather than of planters. The reader needs to know something of the background before meeting the people with whom this book is concerned and who operated against that background. It is odd, however, that the first man whose career needs to be looked at in some detail was not a planter at all but a soldier. He was, indeed, that Sir John Wilson, Commander-in-Chief of the British Forces in

Views of jungle clearing prior to planting in coffee or tea, c. 1867.

47

Ceylon, who has already been mentioned as one of those servants of the Crown who, in the early days, acquired large blocks of land in the island. If the highly condensed version of his story which follows suggests to the reader the plot of a novel produced by the collaboration of Charles Dickens, Mrs Henry Wood and Wilkie Collins, then that is precisely how it emerges from the collection of papers, correspondence and newspaper cuttings which I have been given access to by one of his descendants. Bastardy, insanity, awful secrets and mysterious recluses all appear, together with a faint suggestion of royal involvement.

In its essence, however, the story concerns a will, and it must start, therefore, with some genealogical details. General Sir John Wilson, K.C.B., Knight of the Tower and Sword and Marshal of Portugal, was a member of an ancient Scottish family that had emigrated to Ireland in the sixteenth century. He was born in 1783, the grandson of that Robert Wilson of Augher, Co. Tyrone, whose tomb may still be seen in the graveyard of Londonderry Cathedral. The same Robert Wilson married a second time, by which union he had two further children – Robert the Second and William. William, in his turn, had a daughter, Isabella who married Sir Charles Harcourt Chambers, Chief Justice of Bombay. Robert the Second had a son, James, who, after service in the 84th Regiment of Foot, left the army when peace was declared in 1815 and emigrated to Canada, never to be heard of again.

These details having been established, it is time to revert to the general. His was a romantically unusual career which started when he left Westminster School at the age of eleven to take a commision in the 28th Regiment of Foot, which was the family regiment – a fact that may explain his rather precocious entry into it. He served, as a lieutenant, in the West Indies, was captured by the French at St Lucia when he was thirteen, was exchanged the next year, taken prisoner again on the voyage home, and remained a prisoner this time for no more than a fortnight. In the same year he was castaway on a voyage to Gibraltar, and by 1799, when he was sixteen, he was given the charge of a company in the Minorca Regiment by Sir Charles Stuart. That regiment was engaged, with some distinction, in the Egyptian campaign of 1801, and in 1803, when he was twenty-one, he was given command of a regiment in Ireland on the recommendation of Sir Eyre Coote. From 1805 to 1807, he attended the new Staff College at High Wycombe and came out with a First Class Certificate. In 1809, he was made a lieutenant-colonel and appointed Assistant Adjutant-General in Portugal. The next year he became Inspector of Recruits in the Portuguese Army and was raised to second-in-command under General Libriera. He was badly wounded at the battle of Vimiera, but was fit enough, by 1812, to command the Division of the Minho and to be appointed Military Governor of the Minho. He was wounded, again, at the siege of San Sebastián, and for a third time during the advance into France. After 1815, he retired on half-pay, having inherited a comfortable fortune from his father. Between then and 1830 he lived in London, and apparently occupied himself with various business affairs that considerably increased his fortune. He bought a house in Westbourne Terrace and engaged, as his housekeeper and domestic manager, a certain Mrs Elizabeth Lindsay who was, in spite of her title, unmarried, and who had previously worked as a linen woman at Buckingham Palace.

In 1830, the general was appointed Military Governor and Commander-in-Chief in Ceylon. At the same time he was given the colonelcy of the 11th Regiment of Foot, which, in those days, was worth £1,000 a year as a sinecure. Little is known about his time in Ceylon, where he arrived at the beginning of 1831, apart from the fact that he fought a duel with a certain Sir Charles Marshall in which neither man was scratched, and that he acquired, by grant and purchase, the estates of Peacock, Nilambe and Kalugame. These amounted, originally, to over 5,000 acres, though some of it was later sold to other planters, and much of it was planted, or about to be planted to coffee.

In 1838, General Wilson returned to England and Westbourne Terrace, very much wealthier than when he had left it. He engaged, once again, in business, and increased his fortune by judicious investments in the new railway companies. His Ceylon plantations returned him a steady income which was seldom less than £2,000 a year, and he was able to buy a considerable estate in Wales which he continued to visit periodically until increasing infirmity made travel onerous and, shortly before death, he sold it for £80,000. When he returned, however, from Ceylon, it was to an enlarged household. There was a young boy, George Lindsay Anthony by name, who was accepted as his nephew and whom, in the course of time, he sent to Rugby, Oxford and later into the Guards. The general's mother had married, as her second husband, a certain

Peacock Estate while under coffee. Gampola village in the distance. Note water-mill driven from pelton pipe for the factory, 1864.

Captain George Anthony, so all would have seemed normal had it not been for the fact, subsequently discovered, that in the register of St James's Church, Piccadilly, where the boy had been baptised, the parents' names had been given as General Sir John Wilson and plain Elizabeth Anderson.

Bastardy was no more then than it is now an uncommon thing, and one can accept that the general made the best of it. He must have known that a birth was imminent before he left for Ceylon, since he had arranged for the child to be given one of the family names. In later years, however, it was said that Captain George Anthony was a frequent visitor to the palace, and that he even enjoyed Queen Victoria's friendship. As evidence of this, there hung over his mantelpiece a painting of a dog that had been presented to him by the Queen. Some who knew about these things, and who remembered Elizabeth Lindsay's role as a linen woman at the palace, were not above suggesting that the general may have accepted the boy out of loyalty as a soldier rather than out of a feeling of duty as a parent. Be that as it may, the world in general accepted the fiction that he was his nephew and the fact that he was his bastard.

By 1850, when the general should have been enjoying the peace of approaching old age, his life became increasingly disturbed and unpleasant. Elizabeth Lindsay had become, apparently, a chronic alcoholic and was behaving as drunks were expected to behave in Victorian melodrama. She spent long spells of lonely drinking in her bedroom, punctuating these by sudden descents into the world in order to indulge in painful scenes with the general. Such demonstrations frequently ended in her being turned out of the house, forbidden ever to return. She invariably came back, however, to be reinstated after even more painful scenes of penitence and remorse. George Anthony appeared to ignore completely the woman who was his mother, though he showed considerable respect for the general, who, in his turn, appeared to be proud of Anthony's career as a dashing young officer and a fashionable man about town. Fairly soon, however, Anthony began to show signs of a strangeness of temper that sat ill on a society ornament and an old man's favourite. There was, eventually, a violent quarrel with the general that led to his leaving the house for ever.

Writing about it later, in a letter to a close friend, the general said:

I have indeed to deem myself unfortunate in my domestic arrangements, for of the three inmates of my only home, two have been complete failures – the one acted the Ruffian towards the best friend he had in the world – the other became a confirmed and incorrigible Drunkard. Yet both might, in their respective stations, have been happy and useful and esteemed – had the one not been the victim of a most brutal temper – and the other of a no less brutal vice. But may God give us patience to endure.

That George Anthony soon bitterly regretted what had happened is shown by the letter he wrote, within a few days, from the general's estate in Wales. I quote it in full:

My dear General,

Notwithstanding that it has so recently occurred I feel that it is at least my duty to lose no time in expressing to you my extreme regret and repentance for what took place so unfortunately and so suddenly the other evening, and to apologise most sincerely for the offensive and most ungrateful expressions I believe I used, in a moment of extreme passion and excitement, and to assure you, as you must also be well aware, that in no other way shd. I ever have thought for one moment of making use of them, and indeed I was not able very shortly afterwards to recall to my recollection the words I had used – I trust therefore you will consider it as leniently as you possibly can, and make some allowance for the excitement, I most unfortunately for the moment, allowed to get the better of me, and once more extend to me your entire forgiveness – But however much I may desire a reconciliation, if it is disagreeable to you, I hope at least, *if* we must part, after a friendship of so many years, and the great kindness I have always received at your hands, you will grant me your forgiveness, the last kindness, if you really think that nothing can unite us again, I shall ever have to require of you.

I remain in the earnest hope of a favourable reply from you
Yours Most affectionately
George L. Anthony

P.S. As I have remained here so long, contrary to your orders, I trust you will excuse it, I shall wait most anxiously for an answer ... till Tuesday and on Wednesday I shall take my departure, and I hope with your good wishes for my welfare and success in a career and mode of life I fear I am not very well suited for—

There is no record of this apology ever having been accepted, and the two never met again. The general, it would seem, was unwilling to be insulted by anyone, except, perhaps, Elizabeth Lindsay, with whom he was extraordinarily patient. He had called his man out in Ceylon for an imagined insult, and it was only after they had both stood fire that he accepted his apology. It was impossible for him to call Anthony out, and it was therefore impossible, apparently, to accept his apology. Elizabeth's drunkenness and his own pride now left him isolated in so far as his illegitimate family was concerned. Of his legitimate relations, the only one he had ever shown any regard for was that Lady Isabella Chambers who was his half-cousin. She was, by now, an impoverished widow, and he had gone out of his way to assist her and her children. His interest in them, coupled with his lack of legitimate issue, had more than half persuaded them that they would be his heirs.

The general died in 1856, and his will, when proved, disappointed them. It is true that, among many other generous legacies, he left £10,000 in trust for Isabella and her children, but their interest in the rest of the very large estate was only a reversionary one. Although it had been drawn up after the break with Anthony, he still came into the whole of the personal property, which amounted to over £160,000 as residuary legatee. Furthermore, all the real estate, including the land in Ceylon and the house in London, was left in trust to the same George Anthony and his legitimate heirs. It was only if Anthony died without issue that the estate would pass to Isabella and her issue. Finally, if Isabella's line had failed, then the estate was to pass to that other half-cousin, Major James Wilson, who had disappeared into Canada, and his issue. The general named three of his friends as trustees and executors of his will, and in a codicil added the name of Captain George Lindsay Anthony. One of the friends named as Trustee was a certain John Boustead.

The Bousteads

At this stage it is necessary to break away, for a short time, from the subject of the general's will to consider the Bousteads, who are

53

rather more central to this story than General Wilson or any of his possible heirs. Once again, one has to start to construct a background of family ramifications, but since this is, in essence, a family history, it is not altogether inappropriate to do so.

In 1808, a young man who, to avoid confusion, will be called John Boustead the First, earned his father's displeasure by leading too rackety a life in London. He was bought a commission in the Ceylon Rifles and packed off to the colonies, if not exactly to govern New South Wales, then at least to join in the current campaign against the king of Kandy. After a short interlude, in the course of which he reappeared among his former London haunts because the troopship had been stormbound, he was shipped off once more and arrived, eventually, in Ceylon. He served there for forty years and took part in the pacification of the island. When he retired, in 1843, he was given several large pieces of regimental plate to take back with him to England. He must also have acquired, when they were both on the island, the friendship of General Wilson, for his son, John Boustead the Second, was the trustee mentioned in the will.

This second John Boustead was a partner in the London firm of East India merchants that had originally started as Price & Co. and which had then changed its name to Price, Boustead & Co. The original Price had actually sold the first coffee ever sent from Ceylon, so the connection with the island was a continuing one. John Boustead the Second frequently went out to Ceylon, where he had helped to found the agency firm of Lee Hedges, and had bought several coffee estates. Back in London, he helped found the Commercial Union Assurance Company. He lived in some style, with a grouse moor in the Lake District and the sort of house in Ennismore Gardens that all successful City merchants aspired to. Unfortunately, the firm over-extended itself in its Ceylon ventures. The banking house of Baring Brothers had large interests at that time in Ceylon, and there is an interesting report in the Baring Correspondence from their agents there concerning the reasons for the downfall, in 1879, of Price Boustead:

We see from recent English letters and newspapers that an incorrect impression prevails at home as to the causes which led to the failure of Messrs Price Boustead and Co. . . . They, many years ago, became connected with the Kandy firm of Byrde and

Son, who owned a large number of Coffee Estates in the older districts, of which they became proprietors on Messrs Byrde's failure some ten years ago. Of the Estates a few are still remunerative, others are being worked at a loss, and many at different times have been abandoned. Of those which are still cultivated, few could be realised except at very low prices, as the returns from old Coffee have lately been irregular, and, in consequence of the attacks of the leaf disease, the cost of cultivation has so

Colombo Harbour, c. 1870.

increased that the margin for profit even on the old Estates is greatly reduced. Messrs Price Boustead also came under large advances, apparently unsecured, to the local firm of Rudd Brothers, by whose failure, three months ago, they lost Rs. 250,000. Further, in 1874 or 1875 they lost Rs. 350,000 through the failure of two English shopkeepers.

Mr Boustead invested largely in the District of Morowakorie [*sic*] opened 12 years ago, which for Coffee has proved a complete failure. Some of the Estates are being replanted with Tea, for which the climate and soil are said to be suitable. He purchased from us in 1873 the Delta, Alnwick and Delmar Estates, till then owned by the Countess Gaston de la Rochefoucault (Mrs Cavendish). The first as a Coffee Estate has ceased to be remunerative (the last crop we shipped was 9500 cwts) but we understand the others have fully equalled expectations.

When Price Boustead went bankrupt in 1879, for the reasons mentioned above, coupled with the failure of the Oriental Bank, John Boustead the Second, one of the general's original trustees and now, because of the disappearance of George Anthony (which will be discussed later) and the deaths of the other trustees, the sole trustee of that will, disappears from the story. His son, John Melvill Boustead, however, who had just come down from Oxford, refused to be daunted by the fact that he was suddenly penniless. He managed to get himself appointed receiver for the Price Boustead bankruptcy, borrowed some money from a family friend, and went out to Ceylon. Here he bought himself a partnership in the agency house of Lee Hedges & Co. which his father had helped to set up, offering, undoubtedly, as an inducement, the agency not only of the estates his father had bought, mentioned in the Baring report, but also the agency for the Peacock and Nilambe estates which were then among the best in the island. He did this by virtue of claiming to have taken over, from his father, the sole trusteeship of those estates, which had to remain under his control so long as no one was prepared to claim ownership of them under the will. Trusteeships are not, *ipso facto*, hereditary, and there was no legal basis for his action, but he carried it off and removed the agency for the estates from George Steuart & Co. who had originally been appointed by the general.

In 1886, John Melvill left Lee Hedges and set up on his own in partnership with his brother, L. T. Boustead, who had been planting, and therefore brought considerable field knowledge to the partnership. He took with him, to form the nucleus of the business, the Boustead estates and agency for Peacock and Nilambe, both of which had formed, previously, a not unimportant part of the dowry he had originally brought to Lee Hedges. The new firm of Boustead Brothers flourished. Some part of its success was due to its connections with the Brooks family, who at that time had large estates in Ceylon. Some, however, undoubtedly stemmed from its custodianship of the Peacock and Nilambe estates, a custodianship that amounted, over the next half-century, to something that

Recently opened Colombo to Kandy railway line, c. 1868.

increasingly came to resemble ownership. For the situation was that, until an heir to the Ceylon estates actually emerged, the Bousteads, in their fiduciary situation, real or assumed, could not, without involving themselves in legal liabilities, surrender the estates. And so Peacock and Nilambe continued to be run by the Bousteads as 'trustees for the estate of the late General Sir John Wilson' until the first decade of the next century.

All that needs to be added to the Boustead story at this stage is to record the following facts. In 1880, John Melville Boustead married, in Calcutta, Leila Money, the youngest daughter of that Colonel Edward Money who had been a Kaimakam in the Turkish Army and who had written the *Prize Essay on the Cultivation and Manufacture of Tea in India*. Some years later, L. T. Boustead left the partnership to return to his previous life as a planter. In 1894, Edgar Money, Leila's brother, left the United States, where he had engaged in a number of different activities, to join the firm of Boustead Brothers in Ceylon and, eventually become John Melvill's partner in place of L. T. Boustead.

It is now necessary to return to the problems of General Wilson's will and Captain Anthony's career. This last developed along undeniably eccentric lines. He attended the general's funeral, dealt for a time with the affairs of the estate, and then disappeared. The general's personal estate, which amounted to over £160,000, was administered on his behalf by the family solicitors, and yielded him a substantial income. He refused, however, to take any interest in the real property beyond giving John Boustead the Second power of attorney to deal with the Ceylon estates. As for the house in Westbourne Terrace, he absolutely refused to have anything to do with it and it remained the residence of Elizabeth Lindsay, later Mrs Causzer, until her death. Thereafter it remained empty, though with all the original furnishings in it, until 1910.

A year later, Anthony retired to lead the life of a complete recluse in a hotel in Brentwood. When, thirteen years later, the Commissioners in Lunacy heard of his condition and forced their way into his rooms, armed with a warrant from the Lord Chancellor, they found an apparent lunatic living in a state of indescribable squalor. He had not stirred from his room for several years and, as an article in *The Times* of 24 August 1871 put it:

From wall to wall, and to a considerable height from the floor, the room was literally blocked up with . . . rubbish. Mr A. lay on a small, broken-down sofa in the centre of this mass . . . He was enveloped in a rug and, the Commissioner believes, was without any other clothing. His face was tolerably clean but somewhat pale, his bare arms were lean . . . and very dirty; the nails of both hands of extraordinary length and begrimed . . . he could not walk or even stand up in consequence of recent contraction of his legs . . . His manner was highly nervous, but betrayed no delusions whatsoever . . . He said that he abstained from washing because he found that the use of water aggravated the rheumatism in his fingers. His abstemious living (consisting of only two meals, tea at 5 p.m. and three cutlets with tea or water at 10 p.m.) he explained as expressing his unfavourable opinion of the hotel accommodation . . The atmosphere of the room was very offensive . . . Mr A. owned to the possession of a large income from entailed colonial property . . . managed by a gentle-man holding a high official appointment . . . and of a farm near Brentwood managed by a veterinary surgeon . . . but he had never called on either gentleman to account and neither had rendered any account to him for a very long period . . .

The commissioners had no hesitation in committing him to the Brentwood lunatic asylum as an insane pauper, but he was released from there some months later, either because he was cured or else because he threatened a series of actions to obtain his release. John Boustead the Second, who apparently knew about this, dissuaded the Chambers' family from visiting him, saying that this would merely incense him. When released, he changed his name to Boreham and went to live in Folkestone, where he lived, once again, as a recluse, looked after by a housekeeper, Miss Campbell, and changing house frequently; and since he never sold anything, he finally ended up as a considerable property owner. He went out only at night, and in a bathchair, but seems, on the whole, to have grown into a gentle, extremely charitable, if still eccentric old gentleman. He corresponded constantly with Lady Isabella Chambers and gave considerable financial help to all members of the Chambers family. The only reference he ever made to his past was that he once declared that, 'if pressed to a certain course, he would declare the whole secret, which even Mr Allen did not know'. Since Mr Allen was the family solicitor and accepted the fact that he was the general's bastard as a matter of course, one wonders what secret, real or imaginary, the poor muddled creature referred to.

George Lindsay Anthony, or 'Mr Boreham', died intestate in 1905. By law, the personal estate of a bastard who dies intestate reverts to the Crown, and letters of administration were granted to the Solicitor-General. The *Daily Chronicle* of 18 December printed as headlines to a long article:

Recluse's Fortune. Estate of over £175,000 for the Crown. Disappointed servants.

While the *Daily Telegraph* remarked:

It very rarely happens that so large a sum as this falls to the Crown in similar circumstances in respect of any one estate.

Finally, it has to be recorded that Miss Campbell, Anthony's housekeeper and amanuensis, who had every reason to expect a legacy had a will been made, wrote to one of the Chambers family, all of whom were even more disappointed since they had every reason to expect to inherit both the personal and real property, about John Boustead the Second, who had, by then, been dead for over twenty years:

Yes, Mr Boustead's behaviour was indeed most cowardly and wicked, to betray such trust, for he was Sir J.'s trusted man of business. Mr Boreham [Anthony] used to say if he had only been in better health he would have brought him to book.

She wrote in this vein because the question of the general's real property was still under dispute. That, the reader will remember, was entailed and so did not revert to the Crown as had the personal property. It consisted, by now, of the house in Westbourne Terrace and the estates in Ceylon. The Chambers' children, who were, under the will, the next in line, gained possession of the house, though not of the furniture, which the Crown solicitors insisted was personal property. The position with regard to the Ceylon estates was, however, more complicated. The law of Real Property in Ceylon was based on Roman Dutch law rather than on Common Law, and under this it was possible that the next heirs in tail were not only the Chambers but also the Canadian Wilsons, if any of them could be found. John Melvill Boustead refused to surrender the estates until and unless the succession was finally decided. Moreover, as receiver in bankruptcy of the Price Boustead business, he claimed against those estates for a sum of approximately £20,000, representing capital expenditures advanced by the firm in the course of their long administration.

There now followed five long years of increasingly expensive legal inquiries and litigation. A Canadian lawyer, possibly at Boustead's instigation, came forward with a number of ancient, impoverished and largely illiterate descendants of the Major James Wilson who had disappeared in Canada almost a century earlier. Their proof of descent was based on little more than hearsay and a few family papers, but the Chambers', to their credit, agreed that these were sufficiently authentic to prove the relationship, even though they disputed their right to a share in the estates. John Melvill Boustead, meanwhile, who had long since left Ceylon to open a London office for Boustead Brothers, and who had been followed, in due course, by his partner Edgar Money, fought every inch of the way, contesting the Chambers' rights as sole heirs, refusing to relinquish so long as the question of the Canadian Wilsons remained unsettled, and counter-claiming for the capital advances made by Price & Boustead.

The case for the Chambers family had, ever since Anthony's death, been conducted with great thoroughness and vigour by Theodore Chambers, who was at that time conducting a not over-prosperous business in London called the Electromobile Company Ltd. Acting for the rest of the family, he carried on, for five years, an increasingly complicated legal argument with the Crown, the Bousteads and the Canadian Wilsons. Counsel's opinion was taken almost as regularly as a hospital patient's pulse. Actions were started in the Chancery Court in London and the High Court in Ceylon. Lord Westbury, a member of the board of Theodore's company, conducted a personal investigation of the state of affairs in Ceylon, and by doing so seems to have convinced the Bousteads that he was backing and financing Theodore, which was not, in fact, the case. Finally, in April 1910, Theodore records in a short memorandum the first approaches to a compromise settlement. It runs:

C. D. Rotch, who I knew at the Royal Automobile Club had planted in Ceylon and knew a Mr Money who was J. M. Boustead's partner in Boustead Brothers. Mr Rotch approached Mr

Money to see whether a reasonable compromise could be effected, and he gathered discreetly [*sic*] that Boustead really desired a settlement.

A settlement eventually followed. The Wilsons were bought out. A company was formed to float the Peacock and Nilambe estates as a public company that would buy the land from the Chambers family, payment to be in shares in the new company. The Bousteads, for their part, were to receive one third of the shares in settlement of their claim against the estates and the costs they had incurred in fighting the various claims made against them as trustees. The rubber boom was by then in full swing, and Edgar Money had already demonstrated considerable skill in floating other public companies to take over rubber estates in Ceylon and Malaya, so one may assume that the nature of the compromise came from him. From that time on, Chambers, Bousteads and Moneys were to work together on the boards of various plantation companies in a spirit of friendly co-operation that showed no evidence of having started in the hostility that arose from General Wilson's will and the sad lonely life of Captain George Lindsay Anthony. Much of the credit for this must undoubtedly go to Edgar Money, the first of that family to become a planter in Ceylon.

CHAPTER FOUR

The Plantation Moneys

'Let us now praise famous men, and our fathers that begat us.'
– Ecclesiasticus 44:1

THE pedigrees of human beings are seldom as valid as the pedigrees of race horses or bulls. This may be because we seldom castrate our males and are the only animals who breed haphazardly, in or out of season, with no other witness to our couplings than the blankets. Physical characteristics can be inherited, and so offer some guarantee of an honest begetting, but we do not generally test pedigree against performance and expect a Marathon runner to beget Marathon runners.

It is probably for this reason that geneticists, who are frequently cynical and sceptical people, take less interest in the pedigrees of humans than they do in those of white mice or fruit flies. One of them even went so far as to declare that there can hardly be a true-born Englishman alive today who does not carry in his veins, without even being aware of it, some drops of Plantagenet blood. Be this as it may, there are genealogical tables authenticated by the College of Heralds to prove that the Moneys are descended, on one side of the blanket at least, from Plantagenet kings.

At the beginning of the fifteenth century a certain Henry, Count of Eu and first Earl of Essex, married Lady Isabel Plantagenet, who was undoubtedly descended, through the Duke of Clarence, from Edward III. Around a century and a half later, a distant descendant of Isabel's, William Washbourne of Washbourne, married Hester Ernle. The Ernles of Sussex could not only claim a longer and more legitimate ancestry than any mere descendant of William the Bastard, but they were also related to the almost equally ancient family of the Kyrles of Ross. It was that connection, rather than the

63

tenuous one with the Plantagenets, that was important, since it turned Hester into a great heiress. Her cousin, Constantia Kyrle Ernle, had married the eighth Earl of Kinnoul, and the heir to that union had predeceased her. As a consequence, the rich Kyrle estates of Homme (or Hom) in Herefordshire and Whetham in Wiltshire passed, in the first instance, to Hester, and on her death to her daughter Elizabeth. The effect of all this was that Elizabeth, as one of the greatest heiresses of her time, could expect, in those

Homme House.

days when marriage meant adding title to title, pedigree to pedigree and estates to estates, to choose as her husband almost any member of the great families of the time. In 1723, she married a certain Francis Money of Wellingborough.

If the heralds could confidently trace Elizabeth's ancestry back to the Plantagenets, there was no one who could, with any confidence, decide who Francis Money's immediate parents were. In 1817, Major-General Sir James Money-Kyrle, whom we shall meet later, actually went on a pious pilgrimage to Wellingborough in an attempt to discover his great-grandfather's origins. In a letter to his brother, at that time still merely the Reverend William Money, he writes:

> I hung upon this [sacred spot where his grandfather's remains were deposited] lost in moral reflection for a length of time. It

then occurred to me that I would like to search the Registers and endeavour to find out whether any of Francis Money's ancestors were to be met with.

Nothing, however, could be found. The scent disappeared completely at that point. The pilgrimage may have been inspired by the tradition, still held in the Money family, that Francis had actually brought into the family a fresher and far stronger infusion of royal blood. The story goes that a certain Huguenot refugee called Monnet, who had set up as a weaver in Norwich, had a daughter pretty enough to attract the attention of Charles II at some unspecified stage of his notoriously randy career. The liaison, if such in fact it was, produced no ducal bastards as so many of Charles's more protracted liaisons had done. All that we know is that Francis Money, of unknown parentage, was in possession, a generation later, of the valuable estate of Pitsford in Northamptonshire, and of sufficient influence in high places to be able to claim the hand of one of the wealthiest heiresses in England.

Their grandson, William, who died in 1813, had five sons and two daughters. Two of those sons, James the major-general and William the parson, we have already met. The next, in order of seniority, was George, who particularly concerns us since he was to sire the first of four generations of plantation Moneys. Unfortunately, we know less about George than we do about James, much of whose voluminous correspondence has been preserved. Since we are discussing pedigrees, inheritance and families, it may be worthwhile, therefore, to spend a short while with James in order to discover whether he provides us with any understanding of the Moneys.

It is wrong, perhaps, to expect personal characteristics, other than physical ones, to be inherited, just as it is equally wrong for a writer to nudge his reader in advance in order to tell him what to expect from characters he has yet to meet. Nevertheless, to anyone who has studied the family, James was, in many ways, a typical Money. He was, to judge by his portrait, good looking, and to judge by his letters, extremely articulate. He was sufficiently individualistic to defy the conventions of his age at their most peremptory, when they had to do with the concentration and preservation of property. He seems, above all, to have possessed that quiet self-confidence that springs from a habit of success. All in all, though one should not expect such personal characteristics to be passed on to later generations with all the obvious regularity of a Hapsburg lip or a Guelph chin, it is not unfair to find in James not only the model major-general but also the model Money.

The habit of success which has, in spite of reversals, characterised the plantation Moneys, came perhaps more easily to James than to his descendants. The times were different, death duties had not begun to bite, and his initial success lay in being born the oldest son, and heir, therefore, to William's considerable fortune. His success as a soldier was a more personal affair. His army career, in a warlike period when reputations were easily made and lost, produces no evidence of the brilliance associated with a Wellington or a Moore, but then brilliance must always be a suspect quality never to be preferred to a steady succession of modest successes. James joined the 84th Regiment of Foot as an ensign in 1793. By 1811 he was a lieutenant-colonel in the Recruiting Corps. One cannot imagine that, even in those bloody times, the corps saw much active service. Casualties must therefore have been few, promotion correspondingly slow and a colonelcy difficult to attain. It was undeniably a success to have got as high as lieutenant-colonel. But to end one's career as a major-general in the Recruiting Corps must represent, surely, almost the limit to success that a recruiting officer can legitimately expect.

James was created a baronet in Queen Victoria's Coronation Honours List, was granted the right, by Royal Warrant, to add the name and arms of Kyrle to his own, was made a Deputy Lieutenant and Justice of the Peace for Herefordshire, and all in all may be said to have been as quietly successful in his public life as he had been in his military one.

He died in 1843, leaving no issue. The baronetcy, the double-barrelled name and the estates went to the next brother, whom we have already met as the Reverend William Money. At this point, however, James's unconventionality surfaced. Instead of leaving his large personal fortune immediately, or in reversion, to the next baronet in order to ensure that he and his heirs would have the means to support their new station in life, he left almost all of it to his widow, not in trust but absolutely. It was fortunate, therefore, that the baronetcy lapsed with William's death, five years later.

James's widow, on the other hand, publicly demonstrated her appreciation of his quite unconventional testamentary behaviour by erecting a monument to him in the church at Much Marcle and causing the following inscription to be engraved on it:

SACRED
TO THE MEMORY OF
SIR JAMES KYRLE MONEY
LATE OF HOM HOUSE IN THIS PARISH. BARONET

ELDEST [*sic*] SON AND HEIR OF WILLIAM MONEY
LATE OF HOM HOUSE AFORESAID, ESQ.

HE WAS A MAJOR GENERAL IN THE ARMY AND
MAGISTRATE FOR THE COUNTY OF HEREFORD.

HE DEPARTED THIS LIFE 26 JUNE 1843
AGED 68 YEARS.

IN GRATEFUL REMEMBRANCE OF HIS UNDEVIATING
KINDNESS AND AFFECTION HIS AFFLICTED WIDOW
HAS CAUSED THIS MONUMENT TO BE ERECTED
TO RECORD HER FULL APPRECIATION OF HIS HIGH
INTEGRITY, EXALTED WORTH, AND THOSE MANY
AMIABLE QUALITIES AND UNPRETENDING VIRTUES
WHICH SO PECULIARLY MARKED HIS CHARACTER
AND RENDERED HIM UNIVERSALLY AN OBJECT OF
ESTEEM RESPECT AND LOVE.

She could easily have done less, and have done it less handsomely.

James's correspondence reveals how, even in an age of observant, literate and indefatigable letter-writers, he possessed the gift of eloquence that, a century later, was to descend on Douglas Money and cause any company report he produced, as chairman, essential reading for all City gentlemen. James spent three years, from 1818 to 1821, on the Grand Tour. The letters he wrote to his brother William, whom he had left in charge of his estates, are of particular interest, not only because of their vivid descriptions, their easily flowing narrative, their elegant prose and the success with which he puts anything he wishes to say into words, but also because they voice his opinions on all subjects, from the government of the Papal

William Money.

States to the way in which the battle of Waterloo was fought, with much the same idiosyncratic firmness that Douglas Money was to display when reporting to his shareholders.

Extracts from a letter he wrote after visiting the field of Waterloo will demonstrate what is meant. They reveal, to my mind, more about the battle than any dozen historians have managed to do:

> As I am sure that both Emma and you take an interest in our movements and concerns, I will not delay longer to inform you that Caroline and myself arrived here . . . at Bruxelles and of which place we received very favourable impressions, as a most desirable family residence being particularly healthy and largely supplied with all the necessities and conveniences of life on very reasonable terms and as you will readily suppose we did not whilst there omit to pay due homage to British prowess by a visit to the Victorious and Memorable Field of Waterloo . . . the spot

was admirably well chosen, the immortal Wellington foreseeing a contest on which the liberties of Europe depended. The country is open – the British line extended about three miles from right to left occupying a ridge or elevation which ran along the whole position from which the ground fell or sloped into a gentle valley dividing the English and French lines ... The ground was entirely arable and covered at the time of the 18th of June with heavy crops of wheat beans etc. A circumstance extremely favourable to the English was that a quantity of rain had fallen the day previous to the battle and the land being as in Herefordshire stiff and loamy, the valley became so unsound and miry that it was with great difficulty the Curisiers [*sic*] and French cavalry could make a charge against our position – whilst their horses were kicking and plunging in the boggy ground our Infantry and particularly the Scotch Regiments who have left a most terrific impression on the people of this country advanced upon them ... and made the most dreadful havoc imaginable – A countryman who had been many years in the service of Buonaparte pointed out to me almost with tears in his eyes the fatal spot upon which he said the last effort of the *Old French Guard* was made, and when they were annihilated by a charge of the Scotch Infantry it consisted for thousands of these Troops that there was not a man that fled and that the whole Guard fell on the field of Honour ... I picked up the entire jawbone of some brave fellow who had fallen in his country's cause, which I wrapped up in paper and propose carrying with me to England.

The major-general, though he would undoubtedly have hated the comparison, resembled, in some ways, a famous contemporary of his, that former sergeant-major of the 54th Regiment of Foot, William Cobbett. Like Cobbett, he had a good eye for the lie of the land and the state of the crops. Like him, he had considerable descriptive powers and a sharp, not to say military manner with punctuation. And like him, he had a morbid liking for dead men's bones, for it was Cobbett who dug up Tom Paine's skeleton in America and brought it back to England, only to lose it eventually to, of all people, the Receiver in Bankruptcy. Britain after the Napoleonic Wars may have been a divided and impoverished country trembling on the brink of Revolution, but we cannot today, in our comparative ease and affluence, produce men as individualistic, as eloquent and as essentially English as William Cobbett or Sir James Money-Kyrle.

We have wandered, as perhaps has become customary, some way from the plantation Moneys and their progenitor George. This may be because almost all we know about George is derived from reference to his affairs in letters written by his older brothers James and William. George was born around 1778 and was a lawyer. He went out to India at some unspecified date, but we do know that in 1817 he was married by his brother William, at St George's Church in Hanover Square, London, to Pulchérie de Bourbel, daughter of Ralph Anthony Henry, 6th Marquis de Bourbel Montpinçon. Of the bride, William had this to say:

> Her first appearance was very prepossessing, her figure is good, her face and countenance altogether most pleasing. In addition to this her conversation is lively and sensible and her manner most ladylike, unaffected and decorous. In short she is, in every respect, a most captivating young woman.

The Bourbels of Montpinçon predated both the Plantagenets and the Ernles, for they were created Barons in Normandy in 936. Ralph Anthony Henry, or Antoine Raoul Henri as he was more properly named, had, before the Revolution, been a Colonel de la Garde de la Maison Rouge du Roi, which had not saved him from becoming an émigré. He was granted British nationality under Letters Patent issued by George III in 1797. The titles of count and marquis which he enjoyed as a Frenchman, and which had been granted to his ancestors by Henry III, finally fell into abeyance, for lack of an heir, in 1920. The Château of Montpinçon in Normandy can still be seen, though it is now somewhat dilapidated. It happened to be in the way of the British advance when, in a strange and poetic reversal of history, they took part in the invasion and conquest of Normandy in 1944.

George, as a mere third son, had little or no patrimony to fall back on, and had to earn his own living – a fact that both James and William deplored. Indeed, James wrote sadly to William that George now despaired of being appointed Attorney-General at Calcutta. The previous occupant of that post, who had promised to retire, had suddenly decided to continue. 'In which case,' James wrote, 'George's condition, with an increasing family, will be calamitous.'

If, in the end, George never became Attorney-General, he did at least succeed in becoming a master in equity, Accountant-General and Keeper of the Records of the Supreme Court of Judicature in Calcutta. Moreover, his family increase stopped this side of the calamitous, possibly because Pulchérie, having flirted with danger

The three Money Brothers.

by bearing him five sons, left him. The sons, in order of appearance, were Alonzo, William, George, Aurelian and Edward. Since the Moneys tend to be uxorious but not monogamous, George Senior's separation from Pulchérie was fully understood, even by the Reverend William. He wrote to his wife that he had met George in London in 1836 at Mivart's Hotel, and added:

> He seems to have some impression on his mind that I formed an opinion against him in the case of his separation from Pulchérie. Nothing could be more liberal than his expressions towards her, but he said that they could not live together. I assured him I was not disposed to take either side of the question, but that he should receive Pulchérie in as much as there was no reason whatsoever to the contrary.

Victorian morality may have been about to descend on Britain like a candle snuffer, but nothing could ever prevent one Money being completely liberal about another Money's marital disasters. The next morning the two brothers 'walked to Greenwich Railroad, of which George is a large shareholder, and entering one of the Steam Carriages, we were soon flying at the rate of *23 miles an hour*'.

George was not the first Money to develop connections with India. A cadet branch of the family, the Moneys of Walthamstow,

The providential escape of Major Money.

had long been East India merchants. Robert Money of Walthamstow, who died in 1796, had been a director of the Honourable East India Company. His three sons are depicted in a painting by Rigaud, now in the Greenwich Maritime Museum, looking at maps of India and China, the whole composition being entitled, *The Money Brothers – Three East India Merchants*. There is another painting, by Luny, that also hangs in that museum and which commemorates a famous victory the oldest of the brothers shared in. William Taylor Money had a ship, the *General Goddard*, in the East India Company's service. In 1795 she was waiting at St Helena for the homeward-bound convoy when news came that the Dutch Revolutionary Party had joined the French just at a time when seven Dutch Indiamen were in the neighbourhood of the

island. Money hurriedly armed his ship and set off, in convoy with
H.M.S. *Sceptre* and the *Swallow* packetboat in search of the
Dutchmen. He was the first to make contact with them, and after a
chase he captured the lot. For this he received the thanks of Vice-
Admiral Sir William Essington, a sword from the governor of the
island and a considerable amount of prize money.

Finally, there is another picture, a print this time, that commemorates the exploit of another eighteenth-century Money. It
depicts, fairly crudely, 'The Providential Rescue of Major Money
from the Sea off Yarmouth after having Made an Ascent in a
Balloon from Cantarella Gardens in Norwich on Saturday, the 27th
July 1765'. The major, wearing white tights and a scratch wig, is
shown riding a cotton-wool sea in a most inadequate basin-shaped
gondola that is still attached to his balloon which, like a deflated
conference pear, is dragging over the heads of the anxious sailors in
a cutter who have rushed to the rescue. The major may or may not
have been a relation, though the fact that his family came from
Norwich and knew nothing of its ancestry apart from the fact that it
commenced with a bastardy is not without significance. Moreover,
for those who care to trace family characteristics from one generation to another, it is a fact that the Moneys have always been interested in new inventions and have often been pioneers of fresh
methods of transport. George, as we have already seen, was an early
investor in the railways. His son, the Kaimakam, invented a new
machine for drying tea and evolved and marketed a patent tea manure. In the case of the former, the *Darjeeling News* reported as
follows:

> We alluded recently to Colonel Money's very ingenious plan
> for drying Tea without charcoal. Since then his apparatus has
> been in full work at Soom, and has been inspected by numbers of
> the Darjeeling planters, one and all of whom have, we under-
> stand, reported most favourably on its working. Samples of Tea
> manufacture have been from time to time sent to Calcutta
> brokers for their opinion, and reports have been received from
> fifteen, of whom seven are in favour of Tea made by the old
> charcoal process, seven are in favour of the new furnace process,
> and one reports that the Tea made by each process is exactly the
> same.

Colonel Money is now taking steps to erect his improved furnace, which will be in working order by the end of September, and the whole October crop of Soom Tea will be fired by the new furnace.

Colonel Money has applied for a patent, and as soon as this is granted we hope to give our readers a description of the apparatus. For obvious reasons it would not be advisable to do so before then. We may mention here that one of the most intelligent and practical planters in this district has ordered one of Colonel Money's flues for his private garden.

Of the commercial success of Colonel Money's apparatus we have no doubt whatever, and we trust that Colonel Money will reap a handsome profit from his very ingenious invention, which will be an undoubted boon not only to this district but to all the Tea-producing districts of India.

One point which has struck us as good in Colonel Money's apparatus is that the temperature of the Tea-house is considerably lowered during the firing process as compared with the open chulas and that there is no free carbonic acid gas allowed to escape into the Tea-house, so that those very unpleasant symptoms of slow poisoning which often show themselves in planters and Tea-makers will be unknown in future. At our suggestion Colonel Money has decided to keep a register of the maximum temperature of the Tea-house, whilst the open *chulas* continue in use, and to compare it with the temperature when the new apparatus has superseded them, also to test for free carbonic acid gas in the air with each process.

We are convinced that when the figures are available our readers will be rather astonished at the difference from a sanitary point of view.

On the whole, we think that Colonel Money's invention is by far the most important application of *common sense* and scientific knowledge to Tea manufacture that we have yet seen, and we are almost certain that his apparatus will before long be adopted throughout the Indian Tea districts.

Virtually all tea dryers throughout the world today use the furnace principle. Edward's son, Edgar, helped to bring the first motor car, the first electricity and the first tramways to Colombo, while his grandson, Douglas, in turn owned one of the first motor bicycles in Malaya and was interested, in later years, in new methods of building motor cars. None of this is surprising if one accepts two initial premises. The first is that special attitudes of mind can be and are inherited. The second is that the Money tradition of possessing Stuart blood is soundly based. Charles II, after all, founded the Royal Society and was something of a savant, while his cousin, Prince Rupert, acquired an almost professional reputation as a chemist, alchemist and wizard. Balloons and tramways would certainly have interested both of them.

Sir Alonzo Money.

It is time, however, to return to the five sons Pulchérie bore George Money of Calcutta. Only two of them, William and Edward, directly concern us since they can be described as the first of the plantation Moneys. The others, however, are of slightly more than peripheral interest since they all demonstrate how strong the colonial habit can become in a family, once any member of it has established himself in a colony. A brief look at the careers of the three other brothers would not, therefore, be entirely irrelevant.

The oldest, Alonzo Money, was born in Calcutta in 1821 and died, eighty years later, in Cairo. He had won some fame during the Indian Mutiny by riding across India carrying a large amount of John Company's cash in his saddlebags without losing any of it to the mutineers. He ended his career as financial advisor to the Egyptian government, in which position he must also have saved someone some cash since it earned him a knighthood. He was described as tall, handsome, charming and something of a buck. Even in his later years he was to be seen every day riding a fiery Arab stallion down the Cairene equivalent of Rotten Row, wearing a tall grey hat and quizzing the ladies through an eyeglass fixed into one end of his riding crop. He probably sired a son, Chester, who eventually became the family solicitor. Taken all in all, Alonzo was not an untypical Money.

Aurelian, the third son, was also born in Calcutta, became a soldier, and died, quite young, at the battle of Chillianwalla in 1849. He went into battle, as everyone else did in those decorative but unergonomic days, in a scarlet coat, a black stock and a shako. In the course of the battle he was unfortunate enough to be bowled over by a ball from a native's musket. His shako fell off and rolled away, and he died, not of his wounds, but of sunstroke. He would, these days, have worn camouflaged jungle kit, have been brought to the battle by helicopter and have been evacuated from it by the same vehicle in a matter of minutes. He would not have been allowed to die of sunstroke, but equally, he would not have been allowed to engage in a battle that helped to win and consolidate an Empire.

George, the fourth brother, was, for some unexplained reason, wealthy enough never to need to do anything except pass his time as a man about town in Calcutta and London. He was, like Alonzo, a buck, but differed from Alonzo in being rather short. In that, if in nothing else, he was an untypical Money. He divided his time between India and London, drove his own four-in-hand, was an ardent race-goer and a famous ladies' man. The only occasion on which he showed sign of wishing to take life more seriously was when he abruptly decided that Britain could no longer safely be governed without him. He stood as a parliamentary candidate – though it is not certain for which, if any, party – at a Rochester by-election and was soundly defeated. One has to believe that the Moneys' confidence in their ability to run anything from a rubber company to affairs of state rather better than anyone else had suddenly asserted itself.

Here, then, was a family already equally at home in the colonies and the home country and prepared to fight, play or govern in either of them. We are left, now, to consider the two who were also prepared to be planters. William, the second oldest, was, like his father George, a Calcutta lawyer. He is reputed to have made a fortune at the law and another by a timely investment in cinchona plantations. He suffered, however, from a certain *folie de grandeur* which was evidenced by his willingness to engage in over-grandiose projects and to indulge in what the economist Thorstein Veblen later described as 'conspicuous consumption'. He had his own private train in India as well as in Britain, and never travelled in either country without a retinue of splendidly liveried Indian servants. When in Britain, he made a practice of renting the deer forest of Invermark for the season and would entertain there in a manner that Veblen would easily have recognised.

In the early 1860s, William decided to add to his fortunes by tea-planting. The first tea boom was under way and William indulged in most of the errors his brother Edward was to describe so clearly in the book already quoted. He chose as a site for this venture a remote place in the jungle called Dunagiri, on the border between Assam and Burma. It was not an easy place to reach since it had no established links, either by road or river, with civilisation and the coast. This was the unrealised but fatal flaw in William's plans. Even after the jungle had been cleared and the tea bushes had been planted and eventually brought to harvest, there was still no economic way of getting the crop to market. Dunagiri suffered, as most tea plantations at that time suffered, from a lack of expertise. It failed, however, from a lack of communications.

Yet William, though perhaps unduly sanguine, had not been entirely stupid. Tea in other parts of Assam and Ceylon had brought about improvements in transport that had not even been contemplated when planting first started. The first tea boom was then at its height, and almost any piece of Assamese jungle that was cleared and planted seemed likely to have a road driven through to it before the first bushes came to harvest. It was merely, in his case, that Dunagiri was too far and too isolated for that to happen. William, however, never even contemplated failure. He had, after all, already made two separate fortunes in at least equally uncertain

77

enterprises – at the Calcutta Bar and speculating with cinchona plantations. He was so confident that he would now make a third that he started the venture by giving two hostages to fortune. He sent for his youngest brother, Edward Money, to join him, and he set about building himself a palace. The modest wooden bungalows that most other planters started with seemed to him unsuitable for a Money. He therefore set the local tribesmen to work building him a Xanadu out of the local blue marble. Edward duly arrived, with his young wife, from Hungary – a circumstance to be explained shortly. The jungle was duly cleared and tea bushes planted. The palace, however, was never finished. Long before the jungle finally reclaimed what had been built, it had come to be known, almost inevitably, as 'Money's Folly'.

William need detain us little longer. His style of living combined with the collapse of the Dunagiri venture ensured that there was nothing left of his two other fortunes by the time he died. Since he was a bachelor and had always declared that he would make Edward's oldest son Edgar his heir, the person who was mainly affected was that same Edgar, Thus, once again, that most Victorian of all figures, the disappointed heir, comes into the story. Nevertheless it was probably parental brutality rather than disappointed hopes which drove the young Edgar to Colorado, to work there as a farm labourer and homesteader.

Colorado, however, properly belongs to the next chapter and the succeeding generation of Moneys. What still need to be discussed are the life and times of William's youngest brother, Edgar's father, that Edward James Thrale D'Oyley de Bourbel Money who came out to Assam to make his fortune tea planting, failed to do so, and accordingly wrote a book on tea and how to grow it. However staid, even stodgy, other Moneys may have been, no one who has studied them would deny that the particular group of Moneys just described constituted a colourful generation. Once one begins to study Edward, however, it becomes quite obvious that he was by far the most colourful of them all. Life, someone may or may not have said, imitates bad fiction rather more frequently than bad fiction imitates life. If that is so, then it is quite clear that Edward Money was born to imitate a remarkably bad three-decker novel that, had it ever been written, would have been produced in a highly charged atmosphere as the result of an improbable collaboration between Ouida and G. A. Henty. It is some loss to all future romantic novelists that only what were considered to be the highlights of Edward's career were ever recorded, and these generally by himself. One is left with the suspicion that even his lowlights would have provided inspiration.

Edward was born in Calcutta, the youngest son of George and Pulchérie Money, in 1823. He could have been little more than nineteen years old when he joined the Indian Army since he was

Colonel Edward Money.

only thirty-two when, as a retired officer, he left England with two of his brothers in order 'to go and see the fall of Sebastopol'. Those were interesting days for tourists when one could still travel to the battlefields before and during the battle rather than after it. In the book he wrote about that expedition, *Twelve Months with the Bashi-Bazouks* (Chapman & Hall, 1857, and unfortunately long out of print), he offers no further explanation for the trip, just as he offers no explanation for his sudden decision to take part in the campaign by offering his service to the Bashi-Bazouks.

These were, in fact, an extremely irregular body of native cavalry raised among the various subject peoples of the Ottoman Empire for the purpose of raiding into the Crimea in support of the regular troops campaigning there. The idea had originated in Whitehall, the corps being raised and paid for, on what Money considered to be a ridiculously extravagant scale, by the British government, and commanded and officered by a motley collection of British officers and quasi-officers. It never actually saw service, but during the twelve months that lay between recruitment and disbandment, it led a wild extravagant, colourful life that makes one wonder what might have happened had the Bashi-Bazouks ever taken the field. Yet they are not entirely to be laughed at since they embodied, in many ways, fairly deep-rooted ideas we have about war as a sport that is best understood and enjoyed by amateurs. Any reader who had the good fortune to be connected with any of the private armies thrown up by the war against Hitler will know what is meant. In these, also, the unorthodox and the amateurs predominated, originality always being preferred to uniformity, the gesture becoming almost more important than the campaign.

The Bashi-Bazouks, who had been raised, for the most part, among the Arab and Albanian tribes, were then stationed in Gallipoli. Edward offered to go there from Constantinople to carry dispatches that had come out from England on the same boat as himself. He had already been refused service with the Turkish regular forces, and hoped now to find a place in their irregular ones. His arrival and enlistment are recorded by him in the following simple terms:

'I am extremely obliged to you, Mr Money' [General Beatson, the commanding officer, said] 'for your kindness in bringing these despatches . . . I see, by Captain J . . .'s note that you have been in India. How long were you there? In what Presidency and in what regiment?'

'Ten years', I replied, 'in the Bengal Presidency, and the Twenty-Fifth Regiment.'

'Were you with your regiment the whole time?'

'No, sir. The last six years I held staff appointments in the department of Public Works, though I returned to my regiment for a short time during the Punjab campaign of 1848–9.'

'Ah, you want service with me?'

'I do, sir; and if you have anything to offer me, I shall be thankful for it.'

'Yes, I think I can find something – these pen-and-ink people at home' – striking the papers he had just received – 'send me no end of officers, but they are all paper men – not one in bodily shape have I seen yet – the force might go to the devil if I did not look out for myself. You can ride?'

'I can.'

'Well?'

'If any one with the Duke of Beaufort's hunt questioned it, the sound invariably came from behind.'

'You speak confidently.'

'In seeking service in a cavalry force, I cannot afford to leave you in doubt on such a point.'

'Very well. What rank did you hold in India, or rather do you hold, for I suppose you still belong to the service?'

'No, I left it eighteen months ago. I was very unfortunate in my promotion; and though between thirteen and fourteen years' standing, was but a lieutenant when I left it.'

'Indeed. Well, I will recommend you for a captaincy in this force . . .'

Henty himself could have done no better. Ouida, on the other hand, would have enjoyed his description of the guide allotted him:

My guide, a tall Arab, mounted on a splendid horse, which, by its lean head, large full eye, deep jowl, and small quivering ears, showed its claim to be a true son of the desert . . . rode through quite unconcernedly, smoking his pipe as he did so . . . his peculiar costume consisted of a tightly fitting vest of bright green colour, surmounted by a species of scarlet hussar pelisse, with the sleeves flowing behind; both these garments were richly embroidered in gold, as were also his large loose green trousers stuffed into a pair of yellow boots decorated in front with tassels; covering his head was a gaudily striped silk handkerchief, not twisted as a turban, but tied in a knot at the back of his neck, and hanging like a curtain down his back. Round his waist, or rather stomach, he had a handsome shawl, of apparently Indian manufacture, in which were thrust two clumsy, silver-mounted, flint pistols, as also a 'yataghan' or long knife; at his side dangled a semi-circular sabre; and over his shoulders and hanging behind, he carried a murderous-looking carbine, about seven feet long. His horse was no less richly caparisoned; the head piece was studded with steel bosses or knobs, while from his throat

depended a horse-hair plume, dyed scarlet, two or three feet
long; the reins were brass chains; the saddle, which had a high
peak before and behind was covered with a silver embroidered
cloth, from the bottom of which peeped out his dish-shaped
stirrups, the sharp edges of which are used instead of spurs. I had
forgotten to mention a long ten-foot spear, under the spiked head
of which was attached a round tuft of black feathers. When he
had smoked his pipe he stuck it in his boot, and thus accoutred
he was certainly the most perfect combination of the magnificent,
the warlike and the eccentric that I have ever seen.

Whether Edward Money wrote *Twelve Months with the Bashi-
Bazouks* to record his experiences, to earn some money, or to inter-
vene in an argument – the private army had, like so many others,
ended in a public scandal – no one can tell. What one can say is that
he wrote it extremely well, as I hope the reader will realise from the
short passages quoted. When a man has, as he had, an observant eye,
an argumentative and critical mind, a passionately romantic soul and
an easy flow of language, he is likely to write well. The consequence
is that it is a sufficiently interesting and exciting book to make it
well worth anyone's time to go to the British Museum in order to
read it. And yet it was about very little. He manages to instil some
regular army discipline into his very irregular soldiers. He saves the
life of a Frenchman who is about to be skewered on the lances of
some of those soldiers. He chases deserters, criticises the command
and the War Office, goes on a recruiting march of several thousand
miles, falls ill of a fever and is nursed by a beautiful Greek girl with
whom he falls half in love and about whom, inevitably, he quotes
Byron – and that is about all.

At the end of his year with the Bashi-Bazouks he was raised to
the rank of Kaimakam, or lieutenant-colonel by a Firman signed by
Sultan Abdul Mejid Khan, son of the Sultan Mahmoud-Khan, the
'Always Victorious'. It reads, in the translation available:

Money Bey . . . one of the officers of the cavalry of the Bashi-
Bazouks in the service of the illustrious English Government, he
having displayed in consequence of the knowledge and the
capacity with which he is endowed, most excellent efforts for the
direction and discipline of the soldiers under his command, and
the same having been well attested: I have, in consequence, con-
ferred on the above officer the said rank of Kaimakam. And

according to my supreme will and my sovereign command from which it proceeds, this my revered order has been given from my Imperial Divan decreeing the above mentioned nomination. Written at the commencement of the Month of the Moon of Zil Hididje the year of the Hegir twelve hundred and seventy-two in the Imperial Residence of Constantinople the Well-Kept.

Edward's career as an English and rather Byronic version of Abdul the Bulbul Ameer lasted only twelve months. It ended late in 1856. He was in London, a civilian, and about to marry his second wife in 1858. The surprising thing, however, is that no one knows who his first wife was or where and when he married her. Even the College of Heralds fails to mention her, but proceeds directly to 'im. 2ndly 31 May 1858 Georgina Mary, da. of George Fitzjames Russell of Milltown Park, co Dublin etc.'. Had there been some unmentionable youthful indiscretion? Had he been captured, in India, by the daughter of someone in the Department of Public Works? Had he acquired someone even less mentionable in the Punjab Campaign of '48–'49? Had there been time, in twelve months, to wed and lose the beautiful Greek maid to whom he had quoted 'The Maid of Athens'? When anything can be surmised but nothing can be asserted, all that is left is to agree with old Sir Thomas Browne that, 'What song the Syrens sang, or what name Achilles assumed when he hid among women, though puzzling questions, are not beyond conjecture.'

The Russells, however, and Edward's first meeting with Georgina are adequately documented. They were an old Anglo-Irish family, now somewhat impoverished, who had had to abandon their Irish estates for the then semi-suburban and lesser splendours of Montpellier Square. Edward rode over from his chambers in the Albany to pay a visit, though how he knew about them is not explained. Georgina opened the door. It was love at first sight, with a whirlwind courtship ending in marriage at All Saints' Church, Chelsea. Edward failed, however, to let Georgina or her family know that he was a widower.

As soon as they were married they departed, accompanied by Georgina's older and unmarried sister, to sub-Carpathian Hungary. There Edward was to look after a vast estate that belonged to the Prince Esterhazy, whom he may well have met during his Bashi-Bazouk days. They lived there for a while, in a mixture of barbaric splendour and uncivilised squalor, in a large medieval castle. There was little for them actually to do except feast, hunt and supervise the local peasants, who, though more colourfully dressed, were also inclined to be more wildly behaved than the peasants around Montpellier Square. The odd thing was that it

Mrs Georgina Smythe, previously married to Colonel Edward Money, 1886.

was Edward rather than the two products of the genteel seclusion of Montpellier Square who recoiled from such exoticism. One might have accepted that it was life in India and with the Bashi-Bazouks that had sated him in this respect were it not for the fact that he now eagerly accepted an invitation from his brother William to join him in making a fortune at Dunagiri. It is interesting to note that it was the same sort of invitation that was to bring his son Edgar, thirty years later, from Colorado to Ceylon.

Edward and Georgina accordingly set off on the long, arduous and complicated journey to Assam, and to an even stranger existence than sub-Carpathian Hungary had offered. Emily, Georgina's sister, on the other hand, must by then have acquired a taste for Eastern European exoticism. She departed for Russia, where she spent the next twenty years bringing up young grand dukes and grand duchesses among scenes of even more feudal splendour.

In Dunagiri, separated by several days' journey from any other Europeans, Edward laid the foundations for his future career as an expert on tea, and Georgina laid the foundations for a family. After her first two children, both girls, had been born with no other medical help than the local tribeswomen could offer, she sent home for her two younger sisters. They came out, without the slightest hesitation, not as part of the seasonal 'fleet' that brought hopeful virgins on to the marriage markets of Delhi and Simla, but as two young, inexperienced and unaccompanied women who thought it the most natural thing in the world to plunge into the jungles of Assam merely to support their sister in her procreational duties. Virtue, even in real life, has its own rewards. They both made successful marriages in India and so added, eventually, to the ever-spreading network of Moneys and half-Moneys organising, managing and defending the sub-continent.

Dunagiri, as we know, failed, and Edward, after its collapse, moved to the more settled tea-growing areas around Chittagong. Here he acted as either adviser or manager on various estates, wrote his *Prize Essay*, invented his tea-drying machine, formed a company to produce his patent tea manure and, in various other ways, acted as a tea expert ought to. It is not known, however, whether he ever actually owned and ran a tea estate of his own.

In the end, the family, for which Georgina had produced six children, returned to England and to the lesser exoticisms and greater stability of life in Bognor Regis. There was to be no stability for Edward, on the other hand. In a short while he had run away with another woman, whom he married once Georgina had got a divorce. Like other Moneys before and after him, he tended to regard adultery as a necessary prelude to matrimony. But even now stability eluded him, for, after a few more years, he ran away again with the woman who was to become his fourth and final wife. It is unfortunate that, in this feminist age, one is unable to give the woman's version of all these boltings. We do know, however, that running away from his third wife was not easy. She was a determined woman and she suspected not only what was going to happen but also how it was going to happen.

She crossed to France and took up her station at the Gare de Lyon in Paris with the intention of cutting Edward off as he fled to yet another and wilder shore of love. Since Edward stood six foot seven, was, even in his declining years, strikingly handsome and wore, after the fashion of those days, a beard that reached to his chest, it should not have been difficult to pick him out of a crowd of diminutive Frenchmen. Edward's military training now came to his aid. Having made an accurate estimate of the enemy's intentions, he adopted the most simple of tactics to frustrate them. In short, he shaved off his beard and crouched. Military strategists agree that the simplest, boldest and baldest of movements in the battlefield are generally the ones that succeed. So they did in this case. Edward got away unintercepted. But the baldness, if one may call it that, of his plan brought retribution. The loss of his beard caused him to catch cold. That cold settled on his lungs and brought about the disease from which he eventually died in the highly improbable setting of Worthing. Lady Bracknell, perhaps, would have appreciated the impropriety of such a man dying in such a setting. Worthing was definitely not the place for a man who was a Money, a Bashi-Bazouk, a Kaimakam, a prize essayist and a much-travelled pilgrim of love to choose as a point of final departure.

His final instructions, embodied in his will, were as unconventional as his life had been. He ordered that his body should be cremated in an age when cremation still amounted to an irreligious, if not blasphemous proceeding. Not content with this, he further ordered that his ashes should be buried in the local cemetery, the spot to be marked not by a monument in marble or granite suitably carved and inscribed, but by a simple cairn. Could he have been thinking back to his early days in an India where bodies of the devout were always burnt on a funeral pyre, and where the graves of itinerant holy men were marked by a heap of stones to which every pious passer-by would add at least a pebble?

While Edward was dealing with the problems of his third and fourth wives, the betrayed and deserted Georgina had been having to deal with her own not dissimilar problems. It would seem that those admirable qualities that supported her when she followed Edward from Montpellier Square to Carpathia, and from there to

Dunagiri, that had made it seem natural for her to hunt and kill man-eating tigers, to walk, unarmed, into a lion's den, to bear and rear a large family in the jungle and keep Hungarian and Assamese tribesmen in order were not the qualities needed if she was to hold on to her husbands.

Shortly after her divorce she had, against the family's advice, married a certain Colonel Graham Smyth from North Wales, a region possibly no more civilised than Dunagiri but certainly less remote. It is a commonplace to say that women frequently make mistakes about the men they marry, and there is nothing sexist in that remark since men just as frequently make mistakes about the women they marry. Marriage, in short, is not as sensible an exercise as it ought to be. But some women, and Georgina was one, given another chance and another choice, go on to make exactly the same mistake a second time.

A Kaimakam is, roughly speaking, the equivalent of a colonel. Not all colonels are, of course, bolters. Nevertheless there must be something more than coincidence in the fact that Georgina's two husbands were both colonels and both bolters. One might say that, in all marriages, it takes two to make a bolter, and that the common factor in this case was Georgina rather the colonelcies. But Edward was, as his history shows, a compulsive rather than a compelled bolter, and it is fair to assume that what attracted Georgina to Edward was also what attracted her to Smyth. Be that as it may, the historical fact is that, having returned from a visit to her relations, Georgina discovered that the colonel had bolted, leaving behind him, in North Wales, a securely locked house and not a single word of explanation.

Once again Georgina had to instruct the family lawyers to commence divorce proceedings. Chester Money, Alonzo's putative son, must by then have grown slightly sceptical as he listened, once more, to her assertions that she had always been the perfect and perfectly loving wife. In so far as the absconding Smyth was concerned, she had always, she insisted, done her best for him. Meals had always been carefully planned. The tea and toast had always been piping hot and the fires blazing whenever he came in from his shooting, or whatever else it was that he did in North Wales. Nothing, in short, had ever been left undone to make her adored spouse satisfied and happy. Unfortunately, in the middle of this description of perfect marital harmony carefully attained, she broke off to exclaim: 'The snivelling ass! The dirty blackguard!' Later generations of Moneys have been wise enough to treasure that saying and to use it only when anyone, in or out of the family, has behaved with anything less than perfect propriety.

If the bulk of this chapter has been devoted to describing where the Moneys came from, why they went to India and how they first came into contact with plantation life, then the rest of it must be devoted to introducing those members of that next generation who were to be connected with Ceylon. Georgina, as has been said, bore Edward six children. It is true that only two of them were of any importance in the Ceylon story. Nevertheless, brief references to the other four will, once again, help to fill in the background.

Georgina's progeny fall into two neat categories. Her first three children were girls, and her last three were boys. Norah Money, the oldest daughter, was born in India in 1859 and died in 1950. She obeyed the rules that govern all true Moneys in that she was good-looking, long-lived and not entirely without some qualities of eccentricity. She was also the first of the family to establish connections with Ceylon, though hers were not the important ones so far as this book is concerned. In 1883, she married a wealthy and respected Colombo tea merchant called Villiers Julius, a name, incidentally, that Ouida would have enjoyed. The circumstances of their married life are obscure. It may have been that, as her father's daughter, Norah found matrimony difficult, or it may really have been that Villiers Julius was a moral delinquent badly in need of salvation. The situation must have come to a head when the couple were on leave in England and staying with Norah's brother-in-law, Jack Boustead, in Wimbledon. The unfortunate Villiers was enjoying a cigar and a whisky and soda in the solitude of the garden when a growing noise from outside suggested to him that he might be in some danger of being run down by a brass band. When he rushed into the house to find out what was happening, he was informed that there was, indeed, a brass band outside the garden wall. It belonged to an association known as 'The Virgins of Putney', and Norah, having gathered together all who were both available and eligible, had led them across Wimbledon Common in a great march that had ended at the house in a service of intercession, with brass-band accompaniment, for her erring husband.

The second daughter, Edith, was born at Nani Tai in 1863 and died in 1945. She was, in at least two ways, a true daughter of the

Kaimakam. In the first place, she found it difficult to be satisfied with merely one husband, though in her case she had some reason for dissatisfaction since Colonel Fred Maturin was, by common agreement, the worst-tempered man in all the Indian Army. Since even the most curry-cured of colonels thought Maturin went too far with his outbursts of temper, Edith may be forgiven for agreeing with them.

When, quite reasonably, she ran away from him with another colonel, Maturin, equally reasonably, divorced her. It may seem to the reader, at this stage, that altogether too many bolting colonels have appeared, and that life in the army is not really like that. All the historian can do, however, once he has checked his information, is to present it as dispassionately as he can. He has no more right to be amused than he has to be censorious. Unfortunately for Edith, the particular colonel she bolted with, who was called Porch, died very soon after their position had been regularised by divorce and marriage. He left her, apparently, very little to live on. Whether or not the Kaimakam, that frequently rolling stone, had ever acquired any money of his own cannot be ascertained. He was, after all, the youngest son of a third son himself, and so could have inherited little. It is certainly true, however, that his six children all had to make their own ways in the world, and Edith, with no more colonels to support her, now had to do the same.

Since she was a Money, she was naturally articulate. Since she was Edward's daughter, she had the examples of the *Prize Essay* and *Twelve Months with the Bashi-Bazouks* to lead her astray. In short, she met the challenge of poverty by becoming a professional author – something that, so far as is known, no other Money had ever sunk to. This was still, of course, the age of the novel, and she produced a steady stream of them, all of which, apparently, were published. It is said the the most successful of them all was one called *The Thin Red Line*. This, as the Americans would say, figures. A novelist is never more likely to be successful than when writing out of personal experience. Since she had been married to no less than two colonels, and so, by necessary connection, to two regiments, she could have been doubly successful had she produced a double-decker novel entitled *Two Thin Red Lines*.

The most important of Edward's children, so far as this book is concerned, were Leila, the youngest daughter, and Edgar, the eldest son. Reserving them for the end of the chapter, one is left

with the need to mention the two remaining sons, Aurelian and
Kyrle Money.

Aurelian, the second of the sons, was born at Chittagong in 1868
a few years before the family migrated to Bognor Regis. He was, as
will be seen in the next chapter, one of the principal victims of his
father's bolting tendencies, and was sent out to Colorado at the
tender age of fourteen to make his way in the world. It was here
that he was joined by his elder brother Edgar, and it was here that,

*Aurelian Money, Anne Edmonstone and Edgar Money in Colorado,
U.S.A., 1888.*

within the space of a single year, the two brothers each took as wife
one of the Edmonstone sisters. Aurelian's life thereafter was to be
rather more varied and considerably less successful than Edgar's.
When he failed to make a success at farming, he joined the
Canadian Mounted Police. This cannot have been satisfactory since
he is to be found shortly after working in the United States. It was
here that his wife died, which may have been the reason for his

return to England. Here he married for the second time someone recorded by the College of Heralds as 'Emily, da. of (——) Barton'. The absence of any Christian name for his new father-in-law may or may not suggest a *mésalliance*. Aurelian, at this stage, went into business selling typewriters, a comparatively recent invention that would have appealed to the mechanical and inventive curiosity which surfaces in so many Moneys.

He was, for a time, successful, until the fatal bolting instinct he had inherited took over. He abandoned his second wife in order to run away with his typist, one Lucy Browne. He was married to her, eventually, in 1903, by which time he had sired five children in wedlock and four out of wedlock. It would appear that he resembled his father in being prepared to abandon his progeny when it came to a question of bolting. His was thereafter a life of ups and downs. He was never exactly a remittance man, but Leila had to come to his rescue from time to time and there is little doubt that he experienced considerable poverty before he finally died in 1946.

Kyrle Money, the youngest son, was born in India in 1876 and died in Australia in 1967. There is little to be said about him beyond the fact that he spent part of his career in the Royal Indian Marines and the rest of it breeding and growing gladioli in Australia. His life, one would think, must have been less adventurous than Aurelian's. Gladioli are interesting but not exciting plants. Nevertheless, he lived an adventurous life of the mind which finally found its way into print. It may have been that he was inspired by Edith's successes as a professional writer, or it may merely have been part of the Money inheritance that he, also, should turn to writing towards the end of his life. There existed, at that time, a periodical called the *Wide World Magazine* that specialised in publishing true stories about life in the wilder parts of the Empire and adventures in the outback. Kyrle began submitting stories about his own adventures which continued to be accepted until it became obvious that even a Money could not have had so many different things happen to him in so many different places. In the end the editor had to reject any further exciting instalments. The *Wide World Magazine,* he wrote, had no place for fiction.

Leila Money, Edward and Georgina's youngest daughter, was born at Almorah in the Himalayas in 1865. In 1880, when she was fifteen, she met 'Jack' (John Melvill) Boustead in Calcutta, and shortly afterwards married him. He was, of course, the Boustead we have already met who went out to Ceylon after the failure of Price & Boustead in an effort to restore the family fortune. He had to borrow the money that took him abroad and allowed him to buy an interest in the old-established agency house of Lee Hedges & Co. who had acted as Price & Boustead's agents in the island. He brought them a certain amount of new business, for he not only had the Peacock and Nilambe estates under his control, but also whatever was still viable of his father's many investments in coffee and tea plantations.

By 1886, Jack had prospered sufficiently to be able to sever his connections with Lee Hedges and set up his own agency house. The Wilson and Boustead interests, which he took with him, served as a nucleus for the new business. A year later he was joined by his brother, who had, as a planter, been running the Indurana estate that belonged to the Brooks family. This connection was a valuable one since the Brooks owned no less than eight of the best estates in Ceylon, for which the new agency house, by now called Boustead Brothers, was soon to act. In 1890, the Brooks estates were brought together in a single company called the United Planters' Company of Ceylon Ltd. Boustead Brothers remained agents for this new public company, in addition to which they became large sharehol- ders. It was at this time, when the Bousteads were establishing themselves as an important and profitable agency house, that Jack's brother, L. T. Boustead, chose to leave the partnership and return to planting. There were, by this time, other junior partners in the firm, but Jack felt the need to have some member of the family with him. It could not have been against Leila's will that, in 1892, he wrote to America asking his brother-in-law Edgar Money to join him as an assistant.

Edgar was admitted as a full partner in 1898. Shortly afterwards, Jack and Leila left Ceylon for England. The firm was now suffi- ciently well established for Jack to be able to leave the other part- ners to run it while he returned to England to establish a London branch. This, as has already been pointed out, was always an im- portant step in the development of any agency house. If it was not taken, the business would essentially remain that of a colonial mer- chant and estate agent. If it was taken successfully, it would begin to add to that profitable but limited business an element that would increasingly resemble a London finance house. For it was the London branch, placing its expertise at the service of planters looking for capital and investors wanting to share in the profits of the new tea and rubber plantations, which floated and managed the new public plantation companies that were started almost daily in that period of boom.

Jack Boustead.

Cedric Boustead, his second son, c. 1930.

Jack prospered in London as much as he had in Ceylon. He was, by all accounts, a pleasant and justly popular man about whom possibly only the Wilson connections ever had anything unpleasant to say. He was a good athlete, like so many of the Bousteads, and a good friend and host. What was perhaps even more important was that he was always, or nearly always, a remarkably shrewd business-man. Later Moneys were to say that while the Bousteads contributed shrewdness to the partnership, the Moneys contributed logic. The Boustead shrewdness, they said, was due to a dash of Jewish blood that may, at some time, have come into the Boustead ancestry. The Money logic, of course, came with the French blood of their putative Monnet ancestor. The French, as they themselves confess, are the most logical people in the world. They have Descartes to prove it.

Jack and Leila had five children, of whom two sons, Guy and Cedric, were to be important in the later history of Boustead Brothers. Until Jack's death in 1920, he and Leila lived, so far as can be seen, quite happily, in their large house at Wimbledon. This not only had its own racquets court, but also a room built specially to house what was the second largest privately owned organ in the country. This had to be played cautiously in spite of its special housing. Anyone who played it with all the stops out would shake the entire building to its foundations.

After Jack's death, Leila, true to a Money tradition, married again and married a colonel. He, too, unfortunately, soon left her a widow, albeit a wealthy one. She was now probably the wealthiest member of that particular branch of the Money family, and she took both her wealth and her family seriously. That is to say, she was always ready to give help to such of her brothers and sisters as needed it. One cannot doubt that it was at her suggestion that Edgar, at that time living in considerable poverty as a homesteader in Colorado, was brought across to Ceylon and to his lifetime work in Boustead Brothers. She must have been a kind and pleasant woman, which makes her unpleasant death at the age of seventy-one even more shocking.

She was, in her later years, afflicted with arthritis. As so often happens, that unpleasant disease left her with deformed and largely useless hands. This made her rather more dependent on her maid than she would otherwise have been. In 1936, she was recommended to go to Arizona, whose climate, it was thought, would be of some benefit to her. During the Atlantic crossing, her maid became so sea-sick that it was felt best to send her home immediately. Leila, when she finally arrived in Arizona, found herself in a bath in which she was unable, because of the weakness of her hands, to turn off the hot tap. As a consequence, screaming loudly but in vain for help, she was scalded to death.

Edgar George Money was born at Chittagong in 1866, and later moved with the family to Bognor Regis. Little is known of his boyhood and schooling, apart from the fact that, from the earliest days, he developed an interest in machinery and showed an aptitude for developing mechanical devices that was remarkable in a schoolboy. He was sent, as was quite common those days, to finish his studies at the University of Heidelberg. It was there that he acquired the customary collection of duelling scars, and it was a matter of some dispute in the family as to whether these added to or detracted from his undoubted good looks. Some time in the 1880s, and under circumstances that have never been explained, young Edgar Money went out to join his even younger brother Aurelian in Colorado.

CHAPTER FIVE

From Tea to Rubber

The world's a sea of changes, and to be
Constant in Nature were inconstancy.
– Abraham Cowley: 'Inconstancy'

FEW readers will by this stage doubt that Edward Money, the dashing Kaimakam, was a less than perfect husband to his several wives. According to the reader's temperament, this may or may not be considered a fault in his character. There should be more unanimity, however, about another and more unpleasant fault. He was, it is clear, a less than perfect father to his many children.

The point has to be raised, not to expand the somewhat shadowy picture given of him here, but because the fact that he was, at the best, an indifferent parent was the primary reason why the Moneys remained a plantation family. To elucidate that point, we need at this stage to jump to 1936. That was when Edith Money, his second daughter and the one who sank to novel writing, wrote a letter to Bruce Money, her nephew, who was the oldest son of her brother Aurelian. It is a letter that needs to be quoted almost in its entirety for the situation to emerge. All that the reader needs to remember is that it was written shortly after Leila Boustead, Edith's youngest sister, had met her tragic death in a bathroom in Arizona.

Dear Bruce,

Your father [Aurelian Money] is in a bad way but has forbidden me to tell anyone. But I must. And I write to ask you if you will at once contribute towards his support – anonymously – the only way he would be got to accept it . . . Owing to some obscure wording in Leila's will his entire income has ceased for a period of three months from her death . . . and a small sum now lent to him by Guy and Cedric [Leila's sons] must be repaid out of the £200 that she also left him so that he could leave England if he wished to, or for his entirely penniless [common-law] wife and children at his death. Rather than draw too much on this sum he is trying to live on £1.5.0 a week until the £3 weekly due to him from Leila begins, and this must cover rent, food for five, firing and everything; they are almost starving. It will probably kill him, and his chief anxiety appears to be his wife and his children to whom he is much attached . . .

I've never known, Bruce, why you feel so bitter towards your poor father. And what I'm going to tell you is not done, please understand, with the wish to bring about anything different – for I know he no longer wishes it or would have it.

When my poor, much tried mother [Georgina] at last left my father, when we were all young, our father seemed to take a dislike to us all, and he shipped off to America his little son, aged 14, a very lovable little lad, giving him a fiver and telling him to ask for nothing more. This was Aurelian, your father. He was sent to an awful brute that nobody had ever seen who worked him on his pig farm out there until I believe my unfortunate little brother ran away. And from that day his whole life was one long struggle. When he consented to have you adopted by those who could do so much better for you than he could ever hope to do, I recall his telling me that he would rather have kept you by him, for he deeply felt your mother's [Anne Edmonstone's] death and was very lonely and fond of you. I see no great crime in that. And if he had kept you by him your lot would have been even harder than his own I expect. He may have failed towards you in small ways that I know nothing of, but in giving you up as he did, he thought of your future. Life had hit him hard at an early age and which of us should judge such a case? Are any of us perfect? As regards other things, if you knew all – you'd understand better. His union with Meg has been a faithful one and puts to shame many so-called marriages. They are both utterly devoted to each other and their children and would marry tomorrow if they could.

One thing made Leila and me so happy and proud of him. He shows in his whole appearance and bearing the good blood and ancient lineage that he inherits on both our father's and mother's side. This was not apparent when he was younger. He was a most refined and beautiful looking boy but the rough life and companions out there of course had the inevitable effect in the course of time. But for some reason now in his later years all that has disappeared. His whole bearing is dignified, thoroughbred and what is perhaps even better, good and kind ... I only tell you this because it is right that you should be told. You have disowned him and so, of course, it doesn't really matter. Yet I as his sister feel that I want you to know.

I've spoken to Douglas [Edgar Money's son and the principal character in this history] and he seems much distressed and will go on with what he gave before, but whether Guy or Lorna will do so is doubtful, though I think Cedric will. I've just sent him £1 myself but am myself very hard hit over my darling sister's sudden death and stand to lose £63 that she was sending me in a few days when she met with the accident and died. God knows what I'll do. But I've sent £1 for firing. I can't do more.

Yours Affec.

Aunt Edith

This is, for many reasons, an interesting letter. For the purposes of the narrative, it reveals how unthinkingly, even brutally, the Kaimakam shipped his sons abroad. For the important historical point is that Edgar, his oldest son, soon joined Aurelian in America, and almost certainly for the same reasons. The Moneys may have been an ancient, landed, and on frequent occasions monied family, but the younger sons, and the sons of younger sons, had to find their own ways in the world, generally abroad. Whether they returned, in the end, as remittance men – as Aurelian did – or as Empire builders – as Edgar did – was immaterial to the family though very material to the course of British colonial history.

No person's literary style should be judged on purely epistolary evidence such as this, but one does get from this letter some idea of how *The Thin Red Line* must have been written – as an unpunctuated flow of breathless narrative which was none the less vivid for being artless and none the less veracious for being naïve. The mixture of pity for Aurelian, who had, for the time being, lost his weekly remittance, and of self-pity because £63 had gone permanently astray, the genuine compassion felt for Aurelian's fate as a child and the childish pleasure displayed in his aristocratic appearance in later years all reveal an unself-regarding and uncritical mind that modern writers tend to lack. Apart from the very natural mixture of pathos and bathos in the letter, the discerning reader will have noticed two things. Leila, the only member of the family to have married, in the first instance, money rather than the Army List, looked after her own to the extent of supporting her poorer relations rather more adequately than the Bousteads ever did, though it is true to say that they, though richer, were only Moneys by marriage. The other is how much Bruce Money's position resembled that of Captain Anthony's in reverse. Anthony, in true Victorian fashion, had been disowned by his putative father, General Wilson, while the wretched Aurelian had been disowned by his undoubted son, Bruce. In each case, the reasons for these stern renunciations of natural bonds remain obscure, though it is probable that Bruce, as a child, suffered not so much from being an adopted child as from being passed round, from one great family to another, as some sort of holiday companion for the children of the house – a childhood, in fact, of being constantly *impair*.

Edith, Aurelian and Bruce, however, do not really concern us except in so far as they demonstrate the miseries that occurred whenever a Money departed from the habit of success. The letter has been quoted partly because it throws some light on the character of the Kaimakam, who would otherwise have remained a character in a boy's story book, but mainly because it offers some explanation of how and why the young Edgar Money, like Aurelian, found himself in Colorado.

Almost nothing is known of what Aurelian and Edgar actually did in Colorado, apart from the former's brief stay on a pig farm. The family believes that they worked for some time as farm labourers before acquiring, probably as homesteaders, a farm of their own. The West, at that time, was just as likely to be settled by Britons as by East Coast Yankees, since it still, in some ways, represented 'the colonies', with all that that meant in the way of free land and a fresh start. That this was so is demonstrated by the history of the Edmonstones, a family with which the two Money boys were soon to be connected.

Samuel Edmonstone was a Scottish artist whose seascapes had been sufficiently appreciated in Edinburgh to ensure his election to the Royal Scottish Academy. He lived, in his later years, in the douce suburb of Portobello, where he was an elder of the kirk, which still possesses a stained-glass window that he designed. It was in Portobello that his four children were born, and it was not, in fact, until he was sixty that Samuel thought of emigrating to America. His two sons had done this some years before and had settled in Colorado, and so it was to that state that Samuel and the rest of his family, including his daughters Alice and Anne, moved in 1885. How and when the Money boys met them is not known. What is known is that Edgar married Alice Margaret Edmonstone in 1888, and that Aurelian married her sister, Anne Bruce Douglas Edmonstone, a year later. In the same year, Alice gave birth to Edward Douglas Money and Anne to Bruce Ernle Money. Anne died some time before 1895, since it was in that year that Aurelian remarried, after having left Colorado and joined the Canadian Mounted Police, this probably being a suitable corps in which to recover from the grief of losing his wife. Family tradition, once more, has it that Edgar remained on his Colorado holding, struggling to make a living. A succession of two bad harvests finally ruined him, and in 1892 he accepted a loan of £200 from Jack Boustead, his brother-in-law, the sum being sufficient to cover the costs of moving himself and his family to Ceylon, where a job with Boustead Brothers awaited him.

One is tempted to accept this family account of how the second generation of plantation Moneys arrived in that island, though a slightly different account is given in Sir Thomas Villiers' book, *Mercantile Lore* (Ceylon Observer, Colombo, 1940). Discussing the firm of Boustead Brothers, he remarks, 'E. G. Money [who now joined the firm] had been in business in the United States of America and in Canada for several years, and he introduced considerable business vitality into Colombo.' The reference to business and Canada does not quite match the family story of farming and Colorado, but the details of Edgar's American experiences are largely immaterial. What is important is that he did arrive in Ceylon, did join Boustead Brothers and did introduce considerable business vitality into that firm.

The only question that might be raised is why was he invited to come to Colombo. Leila, as we have seen, looked after her own, Jack Boustead was warm-hearted and Edgar was undoubtedly short of money. That alone could explain the invitation were it not for an important development in the fortunes of Boustead Brothers.

By 1892, Boustead Brothers had become a prosperous agency

house, largely because of its connections with, and holdings in, the United Planters' Company of Ceylon, formed in conjunction with the Brooks family. The very personal nature of business in Ceylon is exemplified by the fact that the Bousteads founded their fortunes on their connections with the Wilson and Brooks families, both of

George Money and Douglas Money, 1891.

them large estate owners. Now, with presumably as much estate work as they could handle, the firm was ready to diversify out of plantations and tea, either on their own or as part of the United Planters' Company. The Colombo Municipal Council had for some time been considering granting a concession for the construction of a tramway system. Bousteads were interested in acquiring that concession. If Edgar Money had no actual experience of tea, other than what he could remember from his Chittagong childhood, all the family knew of his interest in, and skill with, electrical and mechanical machinery, which he had, in an amateur way, been experimenting with ever since childhood. Such a man could be useful to

Bousteads if they branched out into this new venture. There was something more, therefore, than purely family loyalty behind the invitation Jack Boustead sent out to Colorado.

Four years after Edgar arrived in Colombo, the firm of Boustead Brothers was granted the tramways concession. Two years later, in 1898, Edgar Money was made a partner. Since he had no capital so far as is known, it is probable that he had to purchase his partnership on credit, which was one reason, but only one among several, why his partnership account was still heavily in debt at his death.

The construction of the tramways was a large undertaking which led, almost inevitably, to other things like ferry boats and the generation of electricity. The fuller story of the firm is, however, best told through extracts from a speech given many years later by Cedric Boustead, Jack's third son, and by then one of the senior partners, on the occasion of the fiftieth anniversary of the founding of Boustead Brothers. It was given in January 1936 at a celebratory dinner in Colombo. Most of the Boustead business and planting connections attended, as did the chief secretary, Sir Graeme Tyrell. It ended with that customary flow of speeches in which, as an aid to digestion, Englishmen boast, in a deprecatory sort of way, about themselves and their ancestors. Cedric, for his part, had this to say:

I am proud to be able to say that my family has been intimately connected with this Island since the very earliest days of the British occupation, for my great-grandfather . . . came here to join the Ceylon Rifles over 120 years ago. He was out here forty years at a stretch and then retired. He took part in various operations against Kandy . . . An old family portrait [shows] that the Ceylon climate had evidently suited him well, judging from his rubicund countenance which also indicates a certain partiality to a good bottle of port. My grandfather . . . came out here on several visits to the Island. Those were the prosperous days of coffee and he managed to acquire a very considerable interest in this Island besides being the proprietor of many coffee estates Up-country. Amongst his activities he assisted in founding the firm of Lee Hedges and Company and in England he assisted in the founding of that great business, the Commercial Union Assurance Company, which I suppose is one of the largest insurance companies in the whole world.

When the great coffee disease came along his fortune, together with the fortunes of hundreds of other proprietary planters, vanished in the mists of the morning. It will be difficult for many of you gentlemen to realise the appalling poverty which swept over the Island with the coffee smash . . . On the Mount Pleasant Estate in 1879 they were so hard up that they had no money to get to Colombo and had to live chiefly on bananas picked from the jungle . . . the planters in the Kandy district were only able to afford one copy of the *Times of Ceylon* which went round the district.

When the great crash came, my father had just come down from Oxford and found himself penniless. However, a friend of the family, a Sir Henry Peake, came to the rescue and lent him some money with which he purchased himself a partnership in Lee Hedges and Company. He severed his connection with them some years later, and in conjunction with his younger brother . . . the firm of Boustead Brothers was founded on January 1st 1886.

The task of founding the firm . . . was made much easier by the support and assistance given to him by that well-known and old-established firm, Robert Brooks and Company of London. They had had considerable interests in the island ever since the early coffee days and . . . we act as their agents for many estates and companies for which they are London Agents and Secretaries. Our two families were very large shareholders in the United Planters' Company of Ceylon, and our interests in the Island are therefore identical . . .

The family have been connected with the Peacock and Nilambe Estates since 1858, the latter being the oldest estate in Ceylon. They were planted up in coffee by Sir John Wilson who fought in the Peninsular War. He came out to Ceylon in 1813 as Governor and Commander-in-Chief and was granted Peacock lands for services rendered, and the Nilambe lands he acquired at sixpence per acre . . . We are also agents for the highest tea estate in Ceylon and probably in the world – Oliphant. And also for about the best estate in Ceylon – Diyagama East . . .

The firm started . . . in a small office in Queen Street and one must recall that it was largely due to the enterprise of my uncle, the late Edgar Money, who joined the firm in 1892, that electricity was first introduced to this Island. A small lighting set was started at Galle Buck and one of the very first premises to be connected was Queen's House. The Governor of that day was very proud of this new form of lighting and . . . he gave a very large ball soon after its installation. While the dance was in full swing every single light went out. Everything was in confusion – the boys had apparently thrown away the old oil lamps and candles as something quite beneath their contempt. Everyone rushed round in circles, and everyone bumped into each other.

Early imported car, Colombo.

The whole party broke up in confusion. Naturally His Excellency was very angry and everyone in Colombo said that electricity was only a stunt and would never come to anything . . . In spite of the very rapid expansion of electricity and its uses, it was 10 years before the Colombo Electric Tramways and Lighting Company paid a dividend . . . After a few years Boustead Brothers sold the concern to the United Planters' Company who ran it for a few years. Considerable capital was required to lay down the tramway tracks and so The Colombo Electric Tramways and Lighting Company Ltd came into being in 1902. It was found necessary to build a large power station, and so the firm moved to Gasworks Street. The ground was then a swamp and it is interesting to note that during the excavations the remains of an elephant some 500 years old were unearthed.

The Company continued to prosper and in January 1928 the lighting side of the business together with the power station was sold to the Government. The directors did not want to sell. It was a paying business. The only reason ... was to enable the Government to have a free hand in the development of their Hydro-Electric Scheme. They were talking about the Hydro-Electric Scheme when I first came out to the Island in 1912. Twenty-five years have rolled by since then, and they are still talking about it.

The firm also imported the first motor car into the Island – a single cylinder Rover or Humber. It was with some trepidation that Mr Combe decided to try and scale the Ramboda Pass but failed and had to spend the whole night there. He took three days to get to Nuwara Eliya ...

Our planters are second to none and so are our Visiting Agents. One of the great advantages of a comparatively small agency is the fact that a personal touch can be maintained between the planter and his agents not always possible in a much larger concern. My brother and I have often been ragged at the Box and Cox arrangement we have, and for the short periods we stay out here, but in practice this is a most useful arrangement, for it enables us to keep the directors of the companies we represent at Home in touch with affairs in Ceylon, and therefore we have a sort of personal touch between the planters and their directors in London which would otherwise be quite impossible.

That 'Humber or Rover' was actually imported into the island by Edgar Money in 1902, a few years before he joined his brother-in-law Jack Boustead in London to help run the increasingly important London side of the firm. While he had been in Ceylon, he probably never had much to do with the tea-planting side of agency work, but spent a great deal of his time attending to tramways and electric power stations. The Boustead family had, after all, been connected with plantations as owners, planters, agents and merchants for almost a century by then, and it was natural that Jack, and his sons after him, should attend to that side of the business. If it had been physiologically possible, tea would have been in their blood.

What Edgar did acquire, however, apart from some experience with tramways and motor cars, was a certain amount of knowledge about a comparatively new plantation crop – rubber. Since, in the agency firm of Boustead Brothers, tea had, for over half a century, been established as a secondary religion, with members of the Boustead family as its priests, it was natural that Edgar Money, the junior and less experienced partner, should be assigned to look after such rubber interests as the firm began to acquire in Ceylon and Malaya. He was to become, in short, the firm's rubber expert.

Rubber

The history of crops is frequently as fascinating as the history of men, though in practice it is difficult to disentangle the one from the other. Rubber, in terms of years, is one of our most modern crops. Even so, it possesses a history.

When Christopher Columbus returned from his second voyage to the Americas in 1496, he brought back with him, along with many other natural curiosities, a ball made of a solid but resilient material that would, under suitable conditions of temperature, bounce more energetically than any other ball then being used, whether it was a tennis ball made of feathers stuffed into a leather case or one of the inflated pigs' bladders used for football. He described how he had seen the indians on the island of Haiti using it in their games. It was made, they had told him, from a species of gum they obtained from certain jungle trees.

This caoutchouc, as the Spaniards began to call it, aroused little curiosity. There were no obvious uses for it as there were for other vegetable and animal products the explorers were bringing back from the Indies, such as tobacco, maize, turkeys and indian slaves. The Spaniards, moreover, being conquistadores rather than colonists, tended to display little scientific curiosity. They were interested in acquiring what was already known and valued – gold, silver, pearls and souls for Christianity.

Caoutchouc, therefore, which came only from the Spanish and Portuguese colonies in the Americas, remained, for the next two centuries, an object of idle curiosity. It was not until the eighteenth century that the savants of the Age of Enlightenment began to take an interest in it. In 1736, the French mathematician La Condamine went to Brazil in order to measure the arc of the meridian. He returned to inform the world that there were other uses for this new substance than merely bouncing it about. It came in the first instance, he said, from a tall jungle tree called *Hevea brasiliensis*, a member of that very large genus, the Euphorbiacae. It was extracted by the indians as a milky liquid gathered from shallow incisions made in the tree's bark. Each incision yielded only a small amount of this liquid since exudation stopped as soon as the liquid dried sufficiently to seal the incision. When they had gathered enough of it, however, the indians found several uses for it in its liquid state. They painted their cloaks with it in order to make them waterproof. They also made earthen moulds which they coated with the liquid, and when it had dried they were left with crude but waterproof shoes and bottles. In order to turn it into the apparently useless caoutchouc Columbus first brought back to Europe, the indians heated the milky liquid over a fire, stirring it all the time with a stick. When sufficient moisture had been evaporated, they were left with the solid, resilient lump that had first aroused the explorer's curiosity.

By this time it was obvious that the substance possessed properties that were valuable if use could be made of them in the manufactures that marked the beginnings of the Industrial Revolution. The discovery by the Birmingham savant, Dr Joseph Priestley, that lumps of caoutchouc could be used to erase pencil marks did little to widen its use, though it did have two quite different results. It made quite a small lump worth 10s. in the English market, and it gave the substance an English name that has endured. It is called rubber merely because, as Priestley demonstrated, it was by rubbing it across a sheet of paper that pencil marks would be erased. Apart from this, almost the only new use found for the substance was as a handle for surgeons' instruments.

One of the first factory industries to emerge from the Industrial Revolution was the textile industry. It had always been difficult to produce cloth that would remain waterproof for any length of time. Coating the cloth with oil or tar produced oilskins and tarpaulins, but these were both sticky and smelly, and civilians, at least, wanted something better. The concept of marrying rubber and cloth in the manner that La Condamine had reported began to interest manufacturers and chemists. The indians who had produced waterproof cloaks in this way, however, had been able to use rubber in its original liquid state, whereas it could only be brought to Europe as a solid. How could it be turned, once again, into a liquid that could be used for coating or impregnating cloth?

Two French chemists had been experimenting, towards the end of the eighteenth century, with solvents that would bring rubber into a solution. They found that both ether and turpentine would do this, but made no further use of their experiments. It was left to a Scot, Charles Macintosh, and his later partner, Thomas Hancock, to develop the processes that first turned rubber into an industrial raw material. Macintosh found that coal-tar naphtha was a cheap but efficient rubber solvent. Once it was in solution, the rubber could be painted on to cloth, so making it waterproof, but since the surface then remained sticky, he evolved the idea of using two layers of cloth with the rubber solution in between. He shared with Lord Cardigan, the Duke of Wellington and a few other heroes the distinction of having an article of clothing named after him.

Hancock was interested in finding more direct uses for rubber. He wanted to produce a rubber thread that could be incorporated in clothing and footwear. He accordingly evolved a laborious process for cutting thin strips of rubber from the lumps of raw material, but these were difficult to use in manufacture and he was left with a great deal of waste. Since rubber was then a scarce and expensive material, he invented a 'masticator' that would, he hoped, reduce the waste to elastic threads that he could use. The 'masticator' consisted of a hollow wooden cylinder equipped with metal teeth, inside which a smaller spiked cylinder would revolve when a crank was turned by hand. He discovered that this machine produced results the opposite to what he had intended. Instead of reducing the waste scraps to the fine elastic threads he wanted, the friction set up welded them into a single sheet. He had, in short, discovered a way of shaping rubber.

In spite of this it remained a difficult material for industrialists to work with. It possessed, of course, the valuable properties of being elastic, of being able to withstand compression and of being waterproof. On the other hand, it had the disadvantages of perishing comparatively quickly and of behaving differently at different temperatures. In hot weather it was liable to soften and become sticky; in cold it would lose much of its elasticity, harden and crack. These disadvantages were particularly noticeable in a climate with marked extremes of seasonal temperature. The United States had such a climate, and it was an American hardware merchant, Charles

Goodyear, who began to experiment, in the 1830s, with methods of reducing rubber's reaction to temperature changes.

Small rubber industries had, by this time, become established in most industrialised countries, and anything that would make rubber a more stable material to work with would be valuable. Goodyear tried for some time to achieve this result by treating rubber with nitric acid and came close to killing himself in the fumes of his experiments. He then evolved the idea that if rubber could be combined with sulphur, the desired effect would result. The problem was how to bring about the combination. It is said that he was in his kitchen explaining his theories to a friend while holding in his hand the mixture of rubber scraps and sulphur that was perplexing him. An over-exuberant gesture caused him to drop that mixture on to the top of the kitchen stove. Heat did the rest. The sulphur and the rubber combined and he was left with the result he had been seeking: a rubber that perished less easily, that retained its resiliency and that showed a much lower response to changes of temperature.

He later improved the process by adding a little lead to the mixture and gave the resulting product, in the first instance, the name of 'Fireproof Gum'. Later, with an obeisance towards the classics typical of that age, he renamed it 'Vulcanised Rubber', since Vulcan, in the Roman mythology, was the god of fire. It is sad to have to add that Goodyear failed to make a fortune out of his discovery. His rubber manufacturing companies failed. He was forced to spend far too much money in lawsuits protecting his patents and was obliged, before his death in 1860, to spend long periods in a debtor's gaol.

Nevertheless, rubber was now a material manufacturers could work with, and the uses to which it could be put were multiplying. The development of steam power led to a rapidly growing demand for rubber-coated drive belting. Macadamised roads led to a great increase in transport and rubber tyres were found to give a better ride than metal ones. Such tyres were made of solid rubber, even though patents had been taken out for a pneumatic tyre both in England and the United States in the 1840s. The rise in popularity of the bicycle in the last two decades of the century made pneumatic tyres a necessity, and J. B. Dunlop developed his version of them, with marked success, in 1888. Finally, but most important of all, the horseless carriage or motor car was gradually being developed into a serious form of transport. Solid rubber tyres restricted the speed at which it could be driven. Pneumatic tyres removed that restriction.

From now on the motor car was to determine the fortunes of the rubber industry, and the United States was to become, before the end of the century, the centre of the motor car industry. Harvey S. Firestone, a buggy salesman of Detroit, was the only man in that city to run his buggy on pneumatic tyres, a circumstance that led him, in 1895, to start a factory for the manufacture of such tyres. He later went on to produce car tyres, and his friendship with a new Detroit car manufacturer, Henry Ford, led to the rest. Suddenly things were coming together to create an enormous increase in the demand for rubber.

Where, however, was the increased supply to come from? The traditional source of the world's rubber had always been the jungles of Brazil, though a certain amount of wild rubber also came from the Gold Coast, Nigeria and the Congo. Although Brazil doubled her exports of rubber between 1890 and 1900, there were very definite limits to any further expansion. Sending tappers out into the jungle to look for more wild rubber trees to tap is a slow and ultimately self-limiting process. The men who organised the tappers were making Klondike-like fortunes as the price of Para rubber rose to over 4s. a pound on the London market, but, as the demand increased and the price rose, they created the conditions in which competition became inevitable. That competition was to come from plantation rubber.

There was, in Britain, a growing awareness, during the later decades of the nineteenth century, of both the nature and the importance of the rubber crop. It was known that, although there were other trees and plants which produced latex, the milky fluid from which rubber was obtained, *Hevea brasiliensis* was by far the most productive source. It was also known that the tree would only flourish in certain well-defined areas of the tropics, ten degrees north or south of the Equator. Soil type was not a deciding factor, but rainfall was. It would only succeed in areas where the rainfall amounted to a hundred inches or more per annum. This meant, in effect, that it was confined to South-East Asia and some areas of western Africa. It also meant, so far as the Colonial Office was concerned, that it would grow in several of the tropical colonies, including Ceylon, Borneo and Malaya as well as Nigeria and Sierra Leone.

The Colonial Office was not uninterested in discovering new plantation crops for the colonies. The colonies had, as far as possible, to pay for themselves, and the more they could produce in the way of cash crops the more their governments could earn from export duties, land sales and rents. Tea was doing well in Ceylon, but the destruction of the coffee plantations was something that neither the Colonial Office nor the planters would quickly forget. It had impressed on everyone the dangers of monoculture and the necessity for discovering alternative crops in case disease should strike again or markets disappear. Rubber was becoming increasingly valuable as the demand for it increased, but it was, very largely, a Brazilian monopoly, and it was illegal to take seeds of *H. brasiliensis* out of the country. No one, moreover, had tried establishing it as a plantation crop and little was known about where it should be grown and how it would behave if it were domesticated. Accordingly, when H. A. Wickham, the explorer and plant collector, smuggled 70,000 seeds out of Brazil in 1876, the government was very willing to allow them to be planted out in Kew Gardens. Only about 4 per cent of them germinated, but this was enough to allow a large batch of seedlings to be sent to Ceylon and a few to Singapore. None of those sent to Singapore survived and twenty-two more seedlings were sent out the following year, which were planted out in the Residency gardens at Kuala Kangsar in Perak. The rubber plantation industry in Malaya owes its existence to those seedlings, but it is not, in this chapter, Malaya which concerns us.

The seedlings did well in Ceylon, and the young trees were eventually distributed to various plantations for growing on as seed bearers and for testing for rubber production in trial plots. The Ceylon planters were willing to test alternative crops, but were engaged, at the time, in replacing the disastrous coffee plantations with tea, which showed every sign of succeeding. However, tea was still suspect in case it went the way of coffee, and rubber was tried, along with other crops such as cinchona, as a precaution. Some of the estates interplanted it with tea, hoping to establish the trees as a shade crop, while some planted it out in newly cleared land in order to see how it would behave on its own. Tea did too well for any alternative crops ever to be widely adopted, and Ceylon never developed an extensive rubber plantation industry. Nevertheless, when, after long years of dispute between the Bousteads and the

Chambers, the Wilson tea estates were finally floated as a public company in 1910, some 400 of the 4,000-odd acres consisted of rubber planted from 1905 onwards, the oldest of which were already being tapped. The estimated rubber crop for that year was put at 500 pounds which would rise, by 1916, to some 100,000 pounds; and it was thought that, of the unplanted land, some 500 acres was suitable for the planting of 'Para Rubber'.

Edgar Money.

Edgar Money in London

When, at some time between 1905 and 1910, Edgar Money joined Jack Boustead in London, leaving agency work in Ceylon for agency work in the London branch of Boustead Brothers, the rubber boom was in full flood. The early plantings in Ceylon and Malaya were coming into full bearing, the demand for rubber, especially from America, was growing. Its price had gone up to over 6s. a pound, and the London Rubber Market was beginning to prefer plantation rubber to the wild 'Para Rubber' from Brazil, which was all that had come on to the market for almost fifty years.

One consequence of the boom was that rubber plantations, even more than tea estates, began to attract the investor, and most of the plantings in Malaya, which was beginning to emerge as the best centre for the new rubber plantation industry, were made by public companies rather than by private individuals. There was some reason for this, since rubber plantations were, on the whole, more expensive to establish and bring into full bearing than tea estates. This made it difficult for individual planters to survive as estate owners in Malaya, in spite of the fact that official policy was to encourage private ownership and to frown on speculative investments by London-based companies.

Many of the people who invested in the new rubber companies were themselves retired planters or colonial servants who already knew something about the potential profits and risks of rubber planting. What may be called the punting public, however, was brought in by the extremely high returns, both in dividends and capital appreciation, that the few early rubber companies whose plantations were coming into full bearing were reporting. The fact was that Brazil could not increase her rubber production while the American car manufacturers were doubling their car production every two years, sales in that country having increased from 34,000 in 1906 to 187,000 in 1910. Given that situation, the price of rubber could only continue to increase until such time as new plantations coming into production outstripped demand and glutted the market. Since rubber took seven years or more to come into full production, and since, in 1910, the plantations were supplying less than 10 per cent of the world's rubber, the punters had several years to play with. Considering that the few older companies were, by that time, paying dividends of well over 100 per cent and had their shares quoted at somewhere round twenty times their face value, there was scarcely a single new rubber company whose issue of shares was not immediately over-subscribed. Anyone who invested at par in such a company seemed assured of recovering his investment within a few years from a single year's dividends.

Edgar Money must, by that time, have acquired some experience of company formation. His agency work in Ceylon had brought him into contact with the tea companies. He had been in charge of the floating of the Colombo Electric Tramways and Lighting Company, and he had, after his return to England, brought about that formation of the Peacock and Nilambe Tea and Rubber Estates Company that had finally allowed the disputes between the Chambers and Boustead families to be settled.

In 1910, the same year as that particular company was floated, Edgar also floated his first rubber company, the Brooklands Selangor Rubber Company Ltd. In the period between then and 1923, when he died, there were to be many other rubber companies whose formation he successfully arranged, frequently taking his 6 per cent profit as one of the underwriters, and almost always taking a place on the board.

He was not always successful, however, as the case of the Zambos Rubber Company demonstrated. A Dutchman arrived in London in 1911 who succeeded in convincing both Edgar Money and Jack Boustead that he owned a valuable rubber estate in North Borneo which he wanted to sell to the public. Edgar duly floated a company for him and took up a large block of shares for himself. As soon as he got his hands on some of the investors' money, the Dutchman bolted. Edgar, in some alarm, set out for North Borneo to investigate. Since the Dutchman had told him that he had acquired the land for the plantation from the local chief, Edgar thought it prudent to arm himself with gifts. His daughter bred Dalmatian dogs, a popular breed at that time, and so he took two out with him on his long journey to the tribal lands of North Borneo. When he finally arrived at his destination, he discovered that not only had no rubber trees ever been planted, but also that the Dutchman had never acquired any land to plant them on. The chief, however, seemed pleased with the Dalmatians and gave Edgar a young gorilla in return. This bit a sailor as soon as he got it back to his ship and had to be shot before it bit any more. The catastrophe, as can be seen, was a particularly complete one. Edgar lost all his own investment and was, as a consequence, still in debt when he died, twelve years later, and the firm of Boustead Brothers had to reimburse those members of the public who had invested in the legendary Zambos Rubber Plantation.

A few years earlier, in 1908, Edgar's oldest son, Douglas, had gone out to Ceylon to become the third generation of Moneys engaged in the plantation industry. He spent his first year as a 'creeper' or learner on the Peacock estate before going into the

Colombo Group Photograph, 1907. Douglas Money top row, fifth to the right.

Colombo office to learn something about agency work. His father wrote to him offering advice of various sorts about how to behave in Ceylon:

> At all cost, keep out of debt . . . Try and make good friends in Colombo amongst influential people. You will find it will pay you. Get some visiting cards printed and pay a few calls, and remember you must *always* call and leave a card or cards on people who ask you to dinner or to a dance . . .

If, today, this may seem to us somewhat prissy advice to a young man about to become a planter from an old one who had started life as a homesteader in Colorado, there is other, much more important advice and a great deal of kindness and solicitude displayed in some of the other letters. He writes to Douglas to tell him that he will be given a monthly allowance of a hundred rupees to eke out his meagre salary, and he advises him that this should be enough to allow him to live at the Galle Face Hotel while he is in Colombo, which will be better for him than renting a bungalow. He sends him a gun and some clothing and informs him that he has underwritten part of a company issue in his name, that this has earned him £20 which was invested in shares which are now worth £80 and that this will be invested again on his behalf.

Most importantly and most seriously of all, he writes to him about his career. There will, he says, be little future for him in the Colombo office, and he advises him to go to Malaya to get experience of rubber planting. Douglas takes this advice and goes as an assistant at Kampong Kuantan, one of the rubber companies Edgar had floated. Here he does well, for he is put in charge of the whole estate when the superintendent goes on leave. His father writes that he has good reports of his work, and adds:

> You don't know old chap how pleased I was to hear such good accounts of you and to know that you had taken such a keen and willing interest in your work . . . As you have done so well I want to make you a present of something useful. I thought of sending you a motor bike. Would you write and tell me if you would like this or anything else better. If so what kind of motor bike you would prefer – would one of those modern lightweight machines be more useful to you than the ordinary type? They are mostly of 2 to 2½ H.P. single cylinder engines and belt driven and have magneto ignition. In level country I am not sure that they are not the most useful machines as they are handy and light and almost as fast as the heaviest type of machine of 3½ H.P. Of the latter type the Triumph is supposed to be about the best . . .

It is not only the fond parent speaking here, but also the man who imported the first motor car into Ceylon. A year later, however, he is in Malaya himself and writes an indignant letter to Douglas on the subject of money:

> I enclose a bill which has been forwarded to me here and which I consider must be yours as it certainly is not mine. I wish you would promptly pay this also the other bills you left unpaid in Ceylon. I find there are several and they have charged them to me and are dunning me. It has given me a lot of trouble. You certainly should not have run up debts in Ceylon and left without paying them. That sort of thing will never do. You told me also that you were in debt here and were being threatened with law suits. I don't know if you realise that you will ruin your career and prospects and your reputation utterly out here if you go on like this. It seems to me that you are far too extravagant and

careless about money matters. All your work out here and all your ability will be wasted if you do not promptly take a pull on yourself . . .

One wonders whether Douglas ever actually got the motor bike.

The rest of the story belongs, properly, to rubber, Douglas and the next chapter. Edgar died in 1923 after being in the hands of the surgeons in Britain and Germany for over a year. He seems to us the most colourless of the plantation Moneys, but perhaps the kindest and most human. He was, apparently, well liked by his contemporaries, though there was no eccentricity in him. He was not the only Money to be a good businessman, but he may have been the only Money to be only a businessman.

If the rest of the story moves on now to rubber, what is there left to say about Ceylon and tea and the agency house of Boustead Brothers? The period after the Second World War saw the start of that general exodus that ended the old, perhaps anachronistic world of the British tea planter. The tea companies and the agency houses continued, at least for a time, and tea continued to be grown no less efficiently because Sinhalese took over the management of the estates. Indeed, the new Sinhalese managers had a more difficult job to do in the new state of Sri Lanka than their British predecessors had ever had in the old colony of Ceylon. The successive governments, for either political or economic reasons, intervened increasingly in the management of the tea estates, whose profitability was sharply reduced by the heavy taxes levied on tea shipped out of the country. The rapidly growing power of the unions ensured that wages took almost all that was left of the profits of tea growing, while political and racial tensions between Tamils and Sinhalese have made good labour relations on the estates harder to attain. If profits were made, foreign companies found it increasingly difficult to remit them just as it became increasingly difficult to repatriate capital. To those whose estates were, in the end, nationalised, nationalisation may sometimes have come as a relief.

John Money, Douglas's son, belongs to the fourth generation of plantation Moneys, and is probably the last of them who will ever be described in that way. The late Roy Chambers was a descendant of that General Sir John Wilson, K.C.B., Knight of the Tower and the Sword, with whom the Peacock and Nilambe estates originally began; he was also the penultimate chairman of the Peacock and Nilambe (Ceylon) Tea and Rubber Estates Ltd. At the beginning of September 1976, John Money wrote to him:

As you have probably read in the papers, all the tea estates in Ceylon have been nationalised for an abysmal sum payable over five years. It is appalling to believe that the whole of beautiful Peacock should be taken away from the company for the price of one small house in this country. I did try to get permission to build a guest bungalow on the property with some of the compensation money, but this was turned down as being contrary to government policy.

To this Chambers replied a week later:

Nationalisation has been hanging over our heads ever since I joined the Board in 1954 but I do not in the least regret the decision then made to hang on to the Estates as long as we could . . . And so the saga ends nearly 150 years after Sir John's original purchase . . . I fear nationalisation will not assist the Sri Lanka Government's finances nor better the lot of the Tamils . . . sad, very sad . . .

CHAPTER SIX

Douglas Money and Rubber

'Nobility of birth commonly abateth industry.'
– Francis Bacon: 'Of Great Place'

THE aphorisms of essayists, as much as of other sages, are only too often hit-and-miss affairs. If they embody no more than accepted truth, they will amount to little more than platitudes prettily expressed. If they aspire to propound new truths, they will, at the best, be partial ones and lack universality since, as was said in Ecclesiastes: 'The thing that hath been, it is that which shall be; and that which is done is that which shall be done: and there is no new thing under the sun.'

It is certain that Bacon's particular aphorism, whether it discovered new truths or not, would never have applied to Douglas Money. His almost infinitely distant Plantagenet ancestors may have provided him with some claim to nobility of birth, but in spite of that no one, either in Malaya or the City of London, would have agreed that this in any way abated his industry or lessened the labours of a lifetime devoted to rubber.

When a man's entire career is devoted to the industry he serves, his individuality seems frequently to be lost. The industry becomes not only more important but also more interesting than the man, if only because it has subsumed him. This, at first appearance, was the case with Douglas Money. His story was the story of rubber, and it has to be treated as such. Nevertheless, there is evidence that he was no less interesting, no less individualistic, no less a Money than any of his ancestors. One can still, if one wishes, discover inside the planter and company director who devoted his life to the rubber industry that idiosyncratic, even eccentric approach to life which has, I trust, emerged as a dominant Money characteristic.

He was a true Money at least in that he was good-looking, articulate, intelligent, obstinate and completely convinced that he could never be in the wrong. He was, in later years, one of the few men in the City of London capable of exposing both his views and his character in a company report. Of all the vast deserts of words men are capable of creating, none are more lifeless and more arid, more formalised and more featureless, than those normally contained in a chairman's report to his shareholders. Douglas's reports were, by City standards at least, literary, even revolutionary occasions. What emerged from them was not so much a discussion of money expressed in conventional terms of profits, dividends and depreciations as an exposure of Douglas Money expressed in terms of opinions, prophecies and prejudices. There were no company reports like them.

Some of those reports will be discussed as the story of his career in rubber is followed. There is room at this stage, however, for a few more personal clues to his character. Some of them reside in the many anecdotes his family and friends continue to tell about him. I am indebted to his daughter-in-law for the two that follow.

When Douglas went out as a young rubber planter to Malaya, he soon discovered that he was, like almost every other white man in the tropics, becoming a victim of his thirst. For most people, this meant an increasing reliance on alcohol in general and on iced beer and stengahs in particular. Douglas, however, had given up all alcoholic drinks quite early in life. This did not mean that he was any less in need of liquids to restore what he had lost through sweat than the most hardened topers. A long morning's work on the plantation meant dehydration, dehydration meant thirst, and thirst meant a large liquid intake whether alcoholic or not. Douglas found that he had begun to allow his mind to dwell increasingly, throughout those mornings, on the jugs of cold water he would gulp down as soon as he returned to his bungalow.

He found no difficulty in persuading himself that such a dependence was degrading. He had spent most of his childhood with his maternal aunts in Portobello while his parents were in Ceylon, and the Presbyterianism he must have absorbed there may have had something to do with this. A sense of sin is not difficult to find, even today, in Scotland. Whatever the reason for his self-disgust, he suddenly decided that his dependence even on water was unfitting and began to reject the jugs he had so looked forward to. Instead, as soon as he got back from his morning's work, he plunged himself for quarter of an hour into a cold bath. After a few weeks of this discipline, he found that he had finally conquered his thirst and needed no more water to drink than he would have taken in Portobello.

The interesting thing about this particular remedy for thirst is that there is almost no physiological explanation for it. A cold bath would certainly have lowered his body temperature and so would, for a short while, have reduced the amount of moisture he lost through sweat. It would have done nothing, however, to replace what he had already lost, since the human skin is waterproof and cannot absorb bathwater. The relief he got was entirely psychological, a triumph of the will over the sweat glands. It was typical of Douglas's innate obstinacy that he should refuse, in this way, to recognise the quite normal and legitimate claims of his body. His belief in the supremacy of the will could have classified him as a Nietzschean had he not, in later life, developed an interest in psychic research and gone ghost hunting around his Chobham home in the company of Sir Arthur Conan Doyle.

Douglas showed, throughout his life, a strong and quite unconventional passion for building. It is true that any man responsible for the management of an estate will have to develop an interest in building since buildings are an essential part of an estate's machinery. He will generally, however, do no more than decide what needs to be maintained, repaired or put up and leave the technical details to professionals. But this is to ignore the fact that, for some people, a building can be more than a machine and the erection of it can mean something more than good estate management. For such people a building can be a form of self-expression, a method of boasting or a gesture of defiance. What the normal, decent-mannered man cannot say about himself or others in words he may, given the opportunity, say in bricks and mortar.

It is true that Douglas was an articulate man, but he was only so in his public life. If he never held back from commenting, in company reports and in articles and letters in the newspapers, on the sorry state of the rubber industry, the government and the world, it was because he thought it his duty to his shareholders to do so. They were not so much personal statements as *ex cathedra* ones. He made his most important personal statements in the houses he

Kampong Kuantan Bungalow, 'Before and After'. First photograph shows condition of bungalow immediately after end of Japanese occupation.

built. Two of these, in particular, revealed his dogged unconventionality.

The first, a grandiloquent statement for a young man, was made in 1912 when he found himself in charge of his first rubber plantation at Kampong Kuantan. There were at that time no long-established rubber estates, and few of these had been equipped, as yet, for civilised living. This one lacked a suitable bungalow for him to live in, so he promptly set about planning and building one. It was unlike any other of its kind in Malaya. When it was finished it stood six storeys high, and though it is true that almost any house in Malaya is called a bungalow, this was surely stretching that term to its limits. It was built on deeply dug foundations to his own pagoda design. That is, each successive floor was smaller than the one below it, which allowed the ground floor to measure 700 square feet and contain the only indoor swimming pool in Malaya.

He used what was then an unknown material – reinforced concrete – for the foundations and the first three floors, the ingredients having been dug and mixed on the estate. The other three floors were built more traditionally of wood, but every room was enormous and, from his study on the top, Douglas was able to sit at his cards without neglecting his work since he had a panoramic view of most of the plantation and a more specific one of the coolies at work in the rubber.

What was extraordinary about this building as a statement was not so much its exuberance as the fact that it was built, quite successfully, out of almost absolute ignorance. Douglas, who was responsible for it in every detail, knew no more about architecture, construction and reinforced concrete than he had been able to learn from the *Encyclopaedia Britannica*, every one of whose volumes he kept reading and rereading from cover to cover. Young men tend to be confident as well as exuberant, and the bungalow was a notably confident, if not foolhardy statement. The first rubber boom was showing signs of faltering, and no one had yet demonstrated that plantation rubber justified, in the long term, all the speculative hopes placed in it. The entire world trade in rubber in 1912 amounted to no more than 113,000 tons, of which 70,000 tons was wild rubber and only 20,000 tons, as yet, came from the new rubber plantations in Malaya.

One cannot help being reminded of Douglas's great-uncle William, of the fortune he so confidently expected to make in tea,

'Ghost Photographs', 1934. The first picture was taken by time exposure of a modern wooden statue in the hall. No one else was in the
house, and yet the figure on the left appeared in the photograph. The
photograph was taken by Douglas Money, using a Zeiss Ikon camera,
who would certainly have known if someone was standing against the
door post, which was previously the front door post.

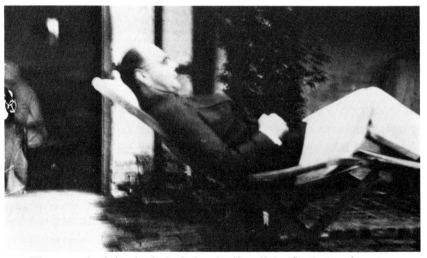

The second photograph includes a view through the garden door,
which is open, into the dining-room. The ghost figure can be clearly
seen sitting in dining-table armchair. Note fold of clothes around
chair leg. The white mark in front of ghost was caused by the pin
which held up negative while drying.
Both photographs were processed by a local chemist. Conan Doyle
satisfied himself of their authenticity.

and of the palace in blue marble he began to build for himself at Dunagiri and never finished. The bungalow-palace at Kampong Kuantan, however, was not only completed: it endured, perhaps for too long. Twenty years after Douglas had left Malaya, the flooring on the ground floor began to lift and buckle. This was in the late 1930s, when intermittent slumps in the rubber industry had made economies essential and were forcing the rubber companies to neglect essential estate work, including land drainage. The then estate manager decided that the foundations must have moved because the subsoil had become waterlogged and reported the bungalow as dangerous. Douglas, back in London, decided that this was nonsense. The *Encyclopaedia Britannica* had said nothing about such a possibility. The Japanese invasion and occupation of Malaya put an end to the argument, but the flooring was still found to be buckled at the end of the war and it was considered prudent to demolish the top three floors to prevent further settling. This was not difficult since they were, as has been mentioned, built of wood.

Some fifteen years later the estate was sold. By that time it had become obvious that there would be no more nabobs requiring even three-storey bungalows in Malaya, and the new owners decided to demolish the building completely. They found that it was impossible to destroy by any ordinary means the concrete put down over fifty years earlier. In the end it had to be blown up, foundations, swimming pool and all. Both Douglas and the *Encyclopaedia Britannica* had been vindicated.

By 1923, Edgar, Douglas's father, was dying slowly of cancer, and Douglas returned to England to take his place in Boustead Brothers and on the boards of the rubber companies. Since he had no house of his own in England, he bought a small black and white medieval cottage in Chobham. It had, he discovered, been one of the original outhouses of Chertsey Abbey, which meant that it had been built, together with the abbey itself, by the monks. This provided some explanation for the apparitions in monks' robes that sometimes manifested themselves and attracted the attention of Conan Doyle. What was even more important, it gave Douglas definite ideas on how to set about his building, for he intended, of course, to extend the cottage in almost every direction.

He argued that the monks who had built both abbey and cottage had not been professional builders. There may have been a craftsman or two among them, perhaps even a mason or carpenter, but most of them had been, so far as building was concerned, laymen. What they had done he could do, especially as he had the experience of bungalow building in Malaya behind him. He accordingly drew up his plans for the first extension and gave them to the local blacksmith to execute. He, though not a builder, was at least a craftsman, which put Douglas in the same position as the monks.

Unfortunately, this was neither medieval England nor the jungles of Malaya, but douce and civilised twentieth-century Surrey. Had Douglas employed an architect or builder, he would have been told that there were by-laws to be observed and sanitary inspectors to enforce them. Neither he nor the blacksmith worried about this, and the first extension, containing a bathroom and lavatory, was added to the cottage. Bathrooms and lavatories need drains, and the only place the drains could lead to was one of the old stewponds, almost two hundred yards from the cottage. A drain was cut, pipes were laid, an outfall was arranged and the whole was backfilled before the sanitary inspector intervened. This, he said, would never do. The by-laws specifically decreed, even in those days before planning had become a religion and when Britain was still imperfectly cocooned in red tape, that every drain leading from a lavatory had to have a stench pipe so many feet high and Douglas's blacksmith had failed to erect one. But, Douglas pointed out, a stench pipe so many feet high would completely spoil the lines of the roof which was so many centuries old. That may be so, the inspector said, and it was greatly to be regretted, but by-laws, after all, were by-laws and were there to be obeyed. The inspector then withdrew and Douglas retired to make an intensive study of the by-laws in question. He discovered that it was indeed laid down that every lavatory drain must have a stench pipe so many feet high, but nothing was laid down to say exactly where, along the line of that drain, it had to be placed. He summoned the blacksmith and ordered him to instal a stench pipe of the correct height at the outfall by the stewpond, where no one could see it and where, of course, it fulfilled no useful function. Neither the inspector nor the council was able to quarrel with the decision, but it seems certain that he must have been the last citizen of Chobham to get away with things in that manner before the by-laws were amended.

Douglas's attitude to authority was never one of mere acquiescence, as his long career demonstrated. He was never reluctant to argue with, question or rebuke politicians and government departments whenever he thought it necessary, nor would he surrender what he considered to be his rights merely because a decision against them had been accepted by everyone else. Once at least, however, he must have pushed those in authority too far, for there exists a letter from the then Home Secretary, dated 26 July 1940 and referring to who knows what dispute, that contains the following magisterial rebuke:

> Sir,
>
> The letter addressed to me on your behalf on the 19th. of this month duly reached me. In my judgement your implied criticism of my Private Secretary is wholly without justification: and, having regard for the amount of public time you have already consumed by unnecessary letters and telephone calls when the subject matter of your correspondence was already receiving due consideration at the hands of those best qualified to deal with it, I must request you to abstain from any further communication with me or my Department on the subject.
>
> I am, Sir,
Yours Faithfully . . .

One wonders whether even this worked.

These anecdotes, trivial perhaps in themselves, seem to me to tell us more about the essential Douglas Money than even the details of his long career in rubber can. What they cannot tell us, however, is anything about the industry he worked in. Since this is, in some ways, a hermaphrodite of a book, concerned not only with a plantation family but also with the plantation industries, it is to the rubber industry that we must now turn.

The Peninsula

The long, complicated and ill-defined history of the Malayan peninsula is hardly relevant to our story. All about it that need concern us is the fact that Malaya, and even more so Malaysia, must be thought of as British-inspired creations of the twentieth century. Although the modern Malayan is himself the product of an apparently unending series of invasions and colonisations by Yunnanese, Siamese, Dravidians, Aryans, Arabs, Sumatrans and Javanese, it was not until 1909 that the entire peninsula was ever brought under anything that resembled unitary control. It was then that the British Governor of Singapore and the Strait Settlements was also named High Commissioner for the Federated and Unfederated States of Malaya.

Ever since Europeans had begun to sail and trade in those waters, they had recognised the strategic importance of the peninsula. Whoever occupied its southern harbours would control the entrances to the Bay of Bengal and the South China Seas and hence the route to the Spice Islands. That was why d'Albuquerque stormed and occupied Malacca in 1511, why the Dutch drove the Portuguese out in 1641 and why the British were able to exploit their ascendancy after the Napoleonic Wars by pressing the Dutch, in 1824, to recognise the peninsula as a British sphere of influence. But the region had always had more than merely strategic value. Although most of it was thick jungle and little except the coast and the river valleys could be settled, it had always produced and traded in goods that other people wanted – gold, tin, pearls, spices, gums, ivory and jungle produce. It was for these things that the Romans had come to what they called the 'Golden Chersonese'. In 1405, the Chinese Admiral Yin Ch'ing led a great fleet to Malacca, then a dependency of Siam, on a mission of goodwill from the new Emperor of China, Chu Ti, and reported that he was able to trade there in tin, ebony, fish and resin. Malacca was later to develop into a great port and the centre of an empire which, if it did not include the whole of the peninsula, did at one time include parts of Sumatra. It was particularly favoured by the monsoon winds, which changed about, with considerable regularity, from season to season, so that the trading junks could come south from China, the prahus north from the islands and the dhows east from the Persian Gulf and the Bay of Bengal, all of them knowing that when the seasons changed there would be favourable winds for their return journeys. It was because of this that ports like Malacca became *entrepôts* for trade brought in by sea from all over a vast region as well as for the produce of the peninsula itself.

When the British established themselves in what became the Strait Colonies and Singapore it was, very largely, in order to benefit from this trade. They came, therefore, as traders rather than settlers and colonists, and they established trading posts and agency houses rather than farms and plantations. The British presence brought in the Chinese in increasing numbers. They also came at first as traders, as they had been doing for centuries, but they also later established themselves as miners and planters, at first only in the Strait Settlements, but later in the nineteenth century spreading northwards into the Malay States.

As miners, they dredged and dug tin from the alluvial soils of the river valleys, and were doing so for at least a century before the first European company was formed to exploit the rich and easily exploited deposits of the mineral in Malaya. After about 1880, there was an increasing demand for tin in the industrialised countries where the use of tinplate for the canning industries was becoming common. But, in addition to mining, the Chinese took to clearing the land of jungle and farming it, wherever they could get permission from the government or the local ruler to do so. They did not, however, farm for subsistence, as they might have done in their villages at home in China. They concentrated, instead, on growing crops such as tapioca, gambier and black pepper for export.

These were all comparatively high-value crops that needed little by way of cultivation and brought quick returns. They tended, however, to exhaust the soil, and so those who grew them had to practise a shifting agriculture. This meant that abandoned plots were left to revert to secondary jungle or lallang grass, something that no government could allow to continue indefinitely. Since most of the Chinese came over, not as settlers, but to make enough money to allow them to return to their native villages, mining the soil in this way seemed to them sensible. What they wanted was a quick return on a small initial investment which they had probably borrowed, in the first instance, from the prosperous Chinese merchant who had financed both their voyage from their home village in China and their requirements in their early days as farmers. Since, however, they worked under something resembling a truck system and were likely to remain in debt to both the village headman and the Singapore merchants for most of their lives, few of them succeeded in returning to their home villages in China. Instead, they remained to provide the labour force for the tin mines and for the shifting agriculture that spread the frontiers of cultivation in the peninsula wider and wider.

If the Chinese in this respect can be thought of as planters in that they cleared and cultivated jungle in order to grow crops *in situ* for perhaps fifteen or twenty years before moving on, few of the early

European settlers imitated them. Most of them, as has been said, were there as traders and merchants. When, in the course of time, they turned to the land as an investment, they wanted something they could occupy on a more permanent basis. They wanted, in short, a freehold whose long-term benefits could be enjoyed by their children and their children's children. They did not want to practise subsistence farming on a communal basis, as the Malays did, any more than they wanted to engage in a shifting agriculture like the Chinese. But it is in the nature of tropical jungle land that its seemingly abundant fertility is rapidly exhausted once it has been cleared and put under cultivation. The humus and mineral nutrients contained in the undisturbed soil are taken up and recycled by the trees and other perennial growths of the jungle, but these are quickly lost through oxidisation and erosion once the soil has been exposed for any length of time to the fierce suns and heavy rains of the tropics. The only safe way to engage in sedentary agriculture under such conditions is to reproduce jungle conditions to the extent of using and recycling the soil's fertility through trees. The problem, therefore, was to discover a tree crop that had an export value, that did not take too long to come into profit, as a timber crop would, and that had not to compete with other, already long-established, tropical plantation crops.

The government in the Strait Settlements was eager to establish a plantation industry since that would provide the revenue with which roads, railways and harbours could be built, which would, in its turn, allow further areas of jungle to be opened up to settlement and cultivation. In this way, a benevolent cycle could be created, and government was willing to initiate such a cycle by providing Europeans with freehold or long-leasehold land, with the beginnings of a communications network, with loans or subsidies, and even with supplies of labour brought in from abroad. The difficulty was to find what crop could trigger off the process.

From the middle of the nineteenth century onwards, a few professional planters began to arrive in the peninsula. The first came from Mauritius and the West Indies and were primarily interested in sugar growing. They established what was for a long time a flourishing sugar industry, mainly in Penang and Province Wellesley, where there was flat, low-lying land suitable for the crop. The next influx of planters came from what may be described as the Ceylon connection. It was, as things go, a fairly long-standing connection since many of the original trading and agency houses in Singapore had been started as branches of Colombo houses. There had even been, since about 1850, a well-established firm in Singapore known as Boustead & Company. This had, at that time, no other connection with the Colombo Bousteads except for having been started by an Edward Boustead who was almost certainly the illegitimate son of the John Boustead who went out to join the Ceylon Rifles in 1808 and to start the Boustead connections with that island. (To make matters even more complicated, Boustead & Company of Singapore eventually became agents for Boustead Brothers of London.)

What *Hemileia vastatrix* had done to the Ceylon coffee industry in the 1870s has already been described. The refusal of many of the planters to believe that coffee, king of all plantation crops, could have failed them has also been mentioned. Some remained in Ceylon, waiting, in vain, for *Hemileia* to pass. Some put their faith in planting the new Liberian coffee which, although lower yielding than Arabica, was believed to be more disease resistant. Others looked for new coffee-growing areas on virgin soils and well away from Ceylon. It was these who, in the main, turned their attention to Malaya.

The coffee boom in the peninsula started slowly with attempts to find the most suitable areas and varieties for cultivation. Arabica, on the whole, proved unsuitable, but the Liberian coffee appeared to flourish in various parts of Malaya and began to be extensively planted. Then, in the late 1880s, slavery was abolished in Brazil and the Brazilian coffee industry fell, for a time, into disarray, just as the sugar industry had in the West Indies for similar reasons half a century earlier. Coffee prices on the London market rose sharply and the Malayan coffee boom took off.

It was, as booms go, fairly short lived. Brazil started to encourage large-scale emigration of peasants from Italy and Portugal, and so found a new labour force, and was able, as a consequence, to resume her domination of world coffee markets. Depradation, not only in the form of *Hemileia* but also in the shape of the caterpillars of the coffee clear-wing hawk moth, *Cephonodes hylas*, began to attack the Malayan coffee plantations. Perhaps the greatest difficulty of all was the fact that the supply of labour in Malaya was insufficient at that time to support a large coffee industry. The native Malays would not willingly undertake plantation work.

The Chinese, who were at home with crops like pepper, gambier and sugar, since they grew these for themselves and were willing to act as contract labour for similar crops on European-owned plantations, had no experience of coffee, which was a capital-intensive crop. The planters who had come over from Ceylon sighed for the Tamil labour they had been accustomed to. They set about recruiting in southern India, but found it was more difficult to persuade Tamils to travel so far afield, especially since the new tea estates in Ceylon were competing for their services.

By the end of the century, the Malayan coffee boom was over. It had, while it lasted, brought about certain highly important changes. A considerable acreage of virgin land had been opened up for plantations. It had been established that soil conditions on cleared land would not necessarily deteriorate if a tree crop was planted. Professional planters had, for the first time, settled in considerable numbers in the peninsula, and the government had accepted the idea of European plantations. The beginnings of a communications system and of a plantation labour force had been established. Since coffee was a capital-intensive crop that needed public investment if it was to be planted on any scale, the London investor had begun to recognise the fact that Malaya and plantation companies offered fresh fields for investment. In the same way, the government in Malaya had begun to recognise the fact that it would be London companies rather than individual planters who would have to be the new landowners, even if this opened the way to frauds and speculators. What was most important of all was the fact that the men who had come as coffee planters from Ceylon had already had experience of the dangers of single crops. Though they had come in order to plant coffee, many of them thought it unwise to plant only coffee. They were willing to experiment with alternative plantation crops such as cinchona, tea and – rubber.

Rubber in Malaya

The seedlings of *Hevea brasiliensis* sent from Kew to Malaya flourished. It was soon established that the peninsula provided better conditions for rubber than Ceylon, just as Ceylon provided better conditions for tea than Malaya. By 1883, the seedlings planted out at Kuala Kangsar were large enough to be tapped, and samples of the rubber were sent to London for testing, the first few pounds of plantation rubber ever to arrive there from Malaya. Seed was also being produced. These were collected, and the first surplus of them was offered to Heslop Hill, the first coffee planter willing to experiment with this new crop.

The 1880s, however, were the years, as we have seen, of the coffee boom. They were also years when rubber prices declined because the output of wild rubber seemed likely to exceed any possible increase in demand. The position was reversed in the 1890s. Coffee slumped, the demand for rubber began to outstrip supplies, and, most importantly, the botanists and the few planters who had started experiments were beginning to discover, by trial and error, how best to grow and harvest rubber in Malaya. The pioneer and evangelist in this respect was the new Director of the Botanical Gardens in Singapore, H. N. Ridley, whose enthusiasm for the crop caused him to be known as 'Mad Ridley' and 'Rubber Ridley', depending on whether he was being discussed by the converted or the heathen.

Rubber began to be planted on a commercial scale in plantations that had originally been cleared for other crops during this decade. Planting was seldom done in pure stands since this was still regarded as too speculative, and it was considered prudent to interplant the rubber in coffee or other crops in order to provide alternatives. The first commercial rubber from Malaya reached London in 1899 and sold for 3s. 10d. a pound. That, more than anything else, persuaded the Malayan government that rubber was indeed the crop they were looking for. It was announced that land would be freely available for rubber planting; that it would bear no more than a nominal rent for the first ten years and only 50 cents an acre thereafter so long as one tenth of the acreage was planted to rubber each year and no other crop was attempted.

In an effort to undo the damage done to the land by the shifting agriculture of the Chinese pepper and gambier planters, it was ruled that any new grants of land made to the Chinese must be used for the establishment of a permanent crop such as rubber or coconuts. Gambier and pepper could only be used as temporary catch crops. The many abandoned gambier and pepper plantations that were now covered with lallang grass were to be offered to potential rubber planters on especially favourable terms.

This, when one considers it, had become the oldest and most

typical of colonial situations. A colonial government was offering free, or almost free, land and the prospects of growing rich from a new crop to anyone prepared to 'adventure' into the wilderness in order to farm it. That, after all, was how the first plantations in Ireland and Virginia had been promoted. The lure of land was still a strong one, and it brought swift responses. In 1897, there were 345 acres planted to rubber in the Federated Malay States. By 1904, this had risen to 19,000 acres. Yet the first plantings had, by that time, only just come to their first tappings, and no one was yet certain about how best to tap, how often and how long tapping could continue, what the commercial life of a rubber tree was, how many of them should be planted to the acre, what cultivations and fertilising were necessary and what labour force would be required. Rubber, in short, was still a matter of faith so far as the planter was concerned, and of hope so far as the investor and the company promoter were concerned. All that was seemingly certain was that the world's demand for rubber was being pushed rapidly upwards by the motor manufacturers, and that the price of rubber on the London market was reacting appropriately. No one knew what the limit to the demand might be any more than anyone knew what the supply, if rubber plantings continued, might amount to. Rubber planting, a new agricultural industry of world-wide importance, was to be based on little more than faith, hope, a sudden sharp rise in demand and memories of *Hemileia vastatrix*. It could, for all anyone knew, have been another South Sea Bubble or a scheme for extracting sunbeams from cucumbers, but the investors remained undismayed: the rubber boom had started.

The Rubber Companies

The calculations made, not only by company promoters but also by official circles, as in the handbook published as a guide for intending settlers by the Malay government, varied considerably in almost everything except the final conclusion drawn, which was that rubber planting would always be highly profitable. Most of them agreed that it would cost between £20 and £40 an acre to plant rubber and bring it to bearing. Most gave a figure for yield, thereafter, of 200 to 300 pounds of rubber an acre. Most agreed that production costs, including bringing the rubber to market, would amount to 1s. per pound. Most agreed that the price, on the market, would fluctuate between 3s. and 5s. per pound. If it fell below 3s., this would knock out the wild rubber producers who then produced the bulk of the world's rubber, and so give unlimited opportunities to plantation rubber. Moreover, at that price the uptake of rubber would increase so rapidly as to make demand outstrip supply, with a rapid rise in price as a consequence. What all this seemed to suggest was that an original investment of at the most £40 an acre would, after six years, give a net return of £50, or at the worst £25 an acre every year from then on. There were indications, during that decade, that these might be over-modest estimations. Rubber averaged over 6s. a pound in 1905, and though it fell to 3s. in 1908, this was put down to the recession in the United States, which normally took 40 per cent of the world crop. Indeed, the price rose sharply the next year and reached the amazing level of 12s. a pound in 1910, to fall, shortly afterwards, to just under 6s.

The profits suggested by these figures were more than sufficient to trigger off an investment boom. It was, one should remember, a period when the British were investing as never before in their colonies. Capital that was no longer wanted for an Industrial Revolution that had run its course was beginning to be one of Britain's principal exports. The investing public had therefore become accustomed to placing its money in strange, exotic places. The retired bank manager living in Wimbledon would not think it strange to split his savings between a gold mine in South Africa, a sheep station in Western Australia, a timber mill in Newfoundland and a tea estate in Ceylon.

That is not to say that all the early investors in rubber companies were retired bank managers in Wimbledon. Rubber was possibly still too much an unknown for such a cautious investor. But a surprisingly large proportion of the middle classes at that time consisted of people who had spent part, at least, of their lives in the colonies. The British educational system was largely occupied in training people for colonial administration. It is probable that the first investors in rubber were retired planters, colonial servants and merchants to whom the names of the obscure Malayan villages that were so often attached to the companies seemed neither strange nor obscure.

The role of the agency houses has already been described, and the Malayan houses were beginning to be larger and more powerful than those in Ceylon. The short-lived Malayan coffee boom had led them, for perhaps the first time, to take an interest in the plantations as agents as well as merchants, and many of the larger ones now switched their attention to rubber. If they had not done so, it seems improbable that the rubber company boom would have taken off in the way that it did. In Malaya, they were the people who knew what proprietary planter was ready to float his estate off on the public, or what blocks of virgin jungle the government was ready to alienate for rubber planting. They were the people who, in London, knew how to put a prospectus together, how to interest the underwriters and larger investors, and how to lend the authority of their name to an offer that might otherwise have gone unheeded. It was, generally speaking, a profitable undertaking in several ways. In Malaya, they might take a profit on first acquiring the land and then selling it to the new company. They would, in any case, draw a fixed fee for their agency work for the company once it was formed, as well as commissions on everything bought and sold on its behalf. In London, they would act as secretary to the new company, might undertake some of the underwriting, might even retain a shareholding, and would probably place at least one member of the agency on the board. The more companies they could float, the more profits they could take. They were therefore slightly more interested in the number rather than the size of the companies, since there was a fixed charge element in everything they did.

Because of this, many of the early rubber companies were small ones: a single proprietary planter, for example, going public in order to be able to retire or because he lacked the capital with which to go over to rubber. The companies might grow much larger in later years, because several of them might have to amalgamate in the bad years in order to be able to survive, or because a particularly large block of land had been granted in one of the native states, or occasionally because a rubber manufacturer like Dunlop or Firestone acquired its own plantations in an attempt to establish some control over supplies and prices. The typical rubber estate in those days, however, would own very few thousand acres and would call on the public for quite small amounts of capital.

Although the large Singapore agency houses – Guthries, Harrisons & Crosfield, Edward Boustead & Company – were the

Douglas Money holding young seedling rubber tree (clearly the best grown) in Kampong Kuantan jungle clearing, 1912.

first and the most active of the rubber company promoters, some Ceylon agency houses were also involved, partly because rubber was being planted, albeit on a smaller scale, in Ceylon, partly because they had taken an interest in the coffee planted in Malaya, and partly because many of the new Malay rubber planters were former Ceylon coffee planters. These, then, were the considerations that led Boustead Brothers to take an interest in rubber companies and to place Edgar Money in charge of rubber in the London office, where, although he died in debt to the partnership, he built up what was eventually to become by far the most important part of the company's business.

There is no need, in a book such as this, to list the large number of rubber firms Bousteads eventually floated. The first of them all was the Kampong Kuantan Rubber Company, which was formed in 1909, although J. M. Boustead had been connected with it when it was still virgin jungle; that is, prior to 1906. It was to this plantation that Douglas Money had gone when he left Ceylon in 1910. Edgar Money, as we know, had written him letters, full of the prudent advice a father should give his son, from the time he arrived in Colombo to the time he was established as a successful deputy superintendent in Malaya.

If you choose to [he wrote in one of these], you can go to the Malay States and get a very good billet on a rubber estate there . . . John Gibson, the Visiting Agent . . . who was one of the owners of Brooklands, which I have just turned into our English Company, when he was at home, recently told me he would give you a good billet if you wanted to go there . . . he was rather anxious that you should go to Brooklands . . . but I told him that I preferred you should go to Kampong . . . Gibson does not pay his S.D.s at all well and I have heard that he works them very hard and is a bit of a 'slave driver'. This entre nous . . . The Brooklands Company was a great success. The shares were enormously over-applied for when issued and . . . are now at a premium of from half a crown to four shillings a two shilling share.

A year later he was to write to him expressing his delight at his success as an assistant and the fact that he was considered fit to act as superintendent during the absence of his superior:

I feel sure that your care of the estate in Irving's absence will fully justify the high opinion he has of you. It seems to me that you will soon be qualified to take over a good Superintendent's billet – if indeed you are not already so and if you think Irving is likely to remain on at Kampong . . . it might be as well if you looked around and kept an eye open for anything of the kind that is going . . . I suggest however that you should be careful what billet you accept, there are so many rotten places – unhealthy and unpopular with labour – very badly opened up and planted and such a billet might be dear at any price – for apart from considerations of health in such cases even the hardest work and most judicious management cannot effect any satisfactory results and proper allowance for this is not always made by employers who do not realise fully the difficulties – and consequently a superintendent's reputation as a good and successful planter and manager is apt to suffer. So it is advisable if possible to get a charge out of which you can really make a success.

In 1911, the visiting agent reported, 'Mr Irving has been unwell for some time back and left on short leave yesterday, Mr Money assuming charge during the interval . . .' In 1912, the Directors' Report said: 'In May last, Mr A. Irving . . . being desirous of retiring, resigned the management of the Estate and Mr Douglas Money, who had been Chief Assistant, was appointed Manager in his place . . .'

The 1913 Report had 'pleasure in recording the Board's appreciation of the services and skill of the Company's Manager . . .' – an encomium that was to be repeated with considerable regularity during the difficult wartime years that were to come. In 1917, the chairman talked of,

The depletion of our European supervising staff, some of our assistants having left to take an active part in the war . . . you owe a great deal to the energy and ability of your manager, Mr Douglas Money. It is not possible for me to speak too warmly of our appreciation of his work and of his services to the Company, especially in this time of war, when experienced assistants are almost impossible to find and managers are badly overworked . . .

In April 1917, Douglas volunteered for active service, and on 23 May was passed by the Selangor Man Power Advisory Board as fit.

Group photograph in Kampong Kuantan Bungalow, 1912. Douglas Money sitting in front of pillar.

The board, however, then went on to record its opinion that:

> Mr Money would serve the interests of his country best in his
> present occupation for the following reasons –
>
> 1) That he is in sole charge of an estate engaged in the cultiva-
> tion of rubber, a product at present of national importance.
>
> 2) That he cannot be replaced.

At the 1920 Annual General Meeting of the company, the chairman, J. M. Boustead, primarily a tea man, paid tribute to his partner, cousin and fellow director, Edgar Money, primarily a rubber
man:

> This Company [he said] has always been a most interesting
> one to me. Its inception was entirely due to the enterprise of my
> partner, Edgar Money, who had gone down to the Straits and
> opened up land there in the days when people had hardly begun
> to think of rubber as the profit-producer it has turned out to be.

The estate had, by then, doubled in size and there was only a small amount of unplanted land still left. A final dividend of 30 per cent was declared making the dividend for the year 50 per cent, and the board recorded its appreciation of the services of Douglas Money who, being on leave for the first time since the war, attended the meeting.

At the 1921 General Meeting, the death of J. M. Boustead was reported and Edgar Money replaced him as chairman. The next year, however, F. A. Govett had to take the chair since Edgar was, by then, too ill to attend. He had started on his long, painful and losing struggle with cancer.

It was because of this that Douglas Money never returned, as a planter, to Malaya. He joined the London staff of Boustead Brothers and was appointed visiting agent for the Kampong Kuantan Rubber Company. The following year he was elected to that company's board, the first of his many appointments as a company director, and became chairman when F. A. Govett died in 1926.

The remainder of this book is concerned with following the course of the rubber industry and of Douglas Money's public life as these were reflected in the fortunes of one of the many rubber companies he was to be concerned with over the next forty years. Those fortunes are recorded laconically and impersonally in such things as balance sheets, company reports, prospectuses, and articles and letters in financial journals. There is little in them to tell us any more about the private Douglas Money than has been told already in this chapter. There is enough in them, however, to allow us, each in our way, to make some estimate of his private character. The estimate I arrive at is the faintly surprising one that he was, like so many of his ancestors, a romantic rather than a realist.

It is surprising because he was a reserved, tightly disciplined man who devoted almost the whole of his life to rubber, whose politics, aspirations, passions and arguments were concerned with rubber, and who has left almost no record of himself that is unconnected with rubber.

Yet this excessive concentration on rubber was, in itself, romantic, and found expression, as one would expect, in romantic ways. Although he was a businessman, he could never get out of the habit of thinking about the problems of rubber as a producer. Any man

Planters, Kuala Selangor district, 1912.
Douglas Money on right.

Group photograph, Kuala Selangor, 1912. Douglas Money second
row, standing.

who has ever spent a part of his life in agriculture is bound to think that way and to be separated, therefore, from his fellows who will, as far as primary production is concerned, think of themselves as consumers. But Douglas was almost morbidly conscious of the weakness of the primary producer in general and of the rubber planter in particular.

He tended to think of the customer – in his case, the tyre manufacturer – as an inevitable opponent rather than as a *raison d'être*. He was always in favour therefore – and this was unusual in a City man in those days – of interventionist policies that would nobble the market and reduce the power of the consumer. In later days, he became especially conscious of the particular weaknesses that attached to the rubber plantation industry. It was subject to speculative booms that could lead to disastrous expansions of the planted areas. It was also subject to the seasonal influences that make it difficult to plan for any continuing stability in any form of agricultural production. He was very conscious of the rubber planter's dependence on the motor industry, and spent much of his time looking for alternative users of rubber, however improbable those might seem. Late in life he became afraid of the substitutes – synthetic rubbers. It is worth noting that the first rubber planter should, if they had followed what was happening in chemical circles, have been aware, from the start, of the possibility of alternatives to plantation rubber emerging. For Isoprene, the basic substance around which the synthetic rubber industry has been built, was first isolated from coal tar by German chemists at about the same time as British botanists were making their first attempts to domesticate *Hevea brasiliensis*.

Douglas was a Money, a company director and a City man. He should, therefore, have had recognisable political responses and have been an ardent supporter of a free market economy. But since he also reasoned as a primary producer, he rejected any dependence, so far as rubber was concerned, on classical liberal doctrines of *laissez faire* and was willing to subscribe to any of the new interventionist theories, whether they were Schachtian or Fabian. There may have been more of self-interest than of romanticism in this, but the vigour of his attacks on those who opposed his views, whether they were colleagues or not, was entirely romantic. So, also, were his constant efforts to find new uses for rubber, which led him into an interest in gadgets and inventions, some of which might have seemed outlandish enough for the White Knight.

Why did rubber mean so much to him? He had, after all, only one year's experience in Ceylon, and the same in Malaya before he was put in charge of a rubber plantation; and since this belonged to a company in which both his father and uncle were directors, it may be thought that he needed to take the situation no more seriously than any other *fils à papa* would have done. Yet, from the first, he showed both an expertise in and an enthusiasm for planting, as well as a willingness to conceptualise about the rubber industry that completely destroy any idea that he was merely the beneficiary of nepotism. One can only adopt the admittedly romantic theory that there was something, either in the Money blood or the Money environment, that encouraged the production of planters.

There is also the problem of his war service, or rather of his absolution from it, to consider. Douglas was twenty-eight when he volunteered for active service. That is, he was still young enough to be a member of the generation that was being systematically destroyed in the trenches. The fact that he volunteered demonstrates his awareness of this. What we do not know is what he felt about being kept back in Malaya when his peers were in Flanders. We do know, however, that he continued to mourn the loss of his younger brother, George, who had replaced him in the firm when he left Colombo, and who had gone from there to die the customary subaltern's death on the Western Front.

To this we must add the fact that he was, when it came to affairs of the heart, quite as romantic, though in a less flamboyant manner, as his Ouidaesque grandfather, the Kaimakam. Colorado, Colombo and Portobello had all been inhibiting influences for a Money. They may have given him habits of reticence and self-discipline that his ancestors would have considered strangely bourgeois. My understanding of him, however, is that these were no more than surface inhibitions. The blood of the Bashi-Bazouk still ran in him.

CHAPTER SEVEN

The Brooklands Selangor Rubber Company

'An honest tale speeds best being plainly told.'
– William Shakespeare: *Richard III*, Act IV, sc. v

T HE purpose of this chapter is a simple one. It is to use the annual reports and balance sheets of a rubber company, stretching over a period of more than fifty years, as a mirror in which the changing fortunes of the plantation rubber industry are reflected. Others that could have been chosen. Brooklands was selected for the following reasons:

(a) It was the second of the rubber companies to be floated by Boustead Brothers, being younger than the Kampong Kuantan company by only a few months.
(b) It always had a Money as chairman.
(c) Its story starts with what was more or less virgin jungle and an infant plantation rubber industry.
(d) It was always a medium-size, moderately successful and conservatively managed company, and so can be taken as representative of the industry at its most stable. It was never as small as Kampong Kuantan was originally, it was never as dangerously speculative as the Waterfall Company was, nor were its estates as widely dispersed over the peninsula as those of the Henrietta Company.

Since, in so far as is possible, it will be told in either Edgar's or Douglas's own words, it will be an honest tale, even though Douglas, an extremely articulate man, may not always tell it plainly. Where reference is made to background matters not mentioned in previous chapters, explanations will be inserted; and where the course of events is made more plain in other documents, these will be referred to. Otherwise the narrative will be allowed to move, jerkily and disjointedly perhaps, from year to year and quotation to quotation.

The Prospectus

This was issued in London on 12 April 1910. It invited investors to subscribe for shares in the Brooklands Selangor Rubber Company Ltd, which had been formed to 'acquire, work and develop the Brooklands and adjoining property known as Olak Limpit or Cromlix Estates, situated in the Langkat District, Jugra, in the State of Selangor, Federated Malay States'.

The company's authorised capital was to be £100,000, split into 1,000,000 two-shilling shares. Of these, 860,000 shares were to be issued at par, 700,000 of which were now offered to the public. The

Shooting at Heppenscombe, 1905. Edgar Money holding gun with butt on ground. Jack Boustead second from right.

remaining 160,000 shares were to be 'issued as fully paid in part payment of the purchase consideration'. The directors were named as Edgar George Money, Director of Kampong Kuantan Rubber Co. Ltd, John Gibson, Planter and Visiting Agent (see previous chapter) and Alfred Reid Venning, I.S.O., late Colonial Secretary, Federated Malay States. The agents, secretaries and registered offices were Boustead Brothers of 3 and 4 Fenchurch Street.

The vendors were described as the Fenchurch Investment Syndicate Ltd, also of 3 and 4 Fenchurch Street, who had agreed to sell the estates to the company for £32,500 plus £3,500 to cover the expenses of forming the company. The syndicate had already entered into the following agreements:

(a) To purchase the Brooklands Estate for £12,000 in cash and £15,000 in fully paid up shares.
(b) To purchase the Olak Limpit Estates for £5,500 in cash.
(c) To pay John Gibson, as one of the original owners of Brooklands, £6,000 in cash and £3,000 in shares out of the sums paid to the Brookland Estate.

NOTE: The situation was a normal one for such transactions. The Syndicate, which was undoubtedly another name for Boustead Brothers, contracted for the purchase of the estates and its sale to the new company at no cost to themselves. The largest of the former estate owners became a shareholder and director. One of the Boustead partners became chairman. The Syndicate took a 6 per cent underwriting commission on the 700,000 shares actually on offer. The directors were to be paid £150 per annum and the chairman £200 per annum plus 2½ per cent of the annual profits.

The total area of the estate was 3,000 acres, with road frontage on two sides. The land was described as flat, free-draining, deep alluvial soil eminently suited to the cultivation of 'Rubber, Cocoanuts [sic] and Coffee'. 'Its suitability for cocoanuts is a special feature of this company.' Of this area, 500 acres had been planted to Para Rubber between June 1908 and December 1909, another 240 acres had been drained and clear felled, 150 were drained and ready for felling while the remaining 2,110 acres were described as 'Virgin Forest'. The planted area had been interplanted with *Coffea robusta* as a catch crop, and the growth of both the rubber and coffee was described by Gibson as 'excellent'.

It is proposed to proceed at once to plant up a further 1,000 acres in Para Rubber. The Directors also have in view the planting of 750 acres in Cocoanuts, for which a portion of the land is reported to be very suitable, and to interplant these extentions [sic] where suitable with Coffee Robusta. Mr Gibson has visited and generally supervised the property since its commencement, and for that reason, and having regard to his reputation as a Rubber Planter and Visiting Agent of Rubber Estates of great experience, the Directors have considered themselves justified in accepting his report, which has since been endorsed by Mr Harvey of Pataling Estate. Mr Gibson (who joins the Board) will act as Managing Director of the Company in Selangor. His estimates of future crops and profits are:

	Rubber Yield lbs.	Profit per lb.	Profit Rubber	Profit Coffee	Total
1911				£362	£362
1912	23,625	3/-	£3,543	£1,117	£4,660
1913	68,200	2/6	£8,525	£1,995	£10,520
1914	178,250	2/6	£22,280	£3,025	£25,305
1915	207,250	2/3	£36,674	£3,355	£40,020
1916	257,250	2/-	£45,725	£3,355	£49,080

The present issue will, it is estimated, make available the sum of £43,000 for working Capital for the purposes of the planted acreage, and it is estimated that this sum should also be sufficient to carry out the programme of extensions above referred to. There is established on the property a good Tamil labour force, and steps are being taken in anticipation of the extensions contemplated, to increase the same. There is also always available plenty of Malay labour for felling and draining work, a Malay Village being opposite to the property, and Malay labour in this neighbourhood being abundant. The health of the labour force is excellent, and the district is generally a very healthy one.

NOTE: Although the rubber boom had resumed, after its temporary halt in 1906, it is clear that this still represented a cautious approach to the crop, with coffee and coconuts providing alternatives that could or could not be chosen. The profit estimates for rubber clearly allow for tapping expenses to rise as increasing numbers of immature trees had to be tapped. The calculation was probably based on a market price of 4s. a pound and production costs of 1s. a pound rising to 2s. as the proportion of young trees increased. The distinction between Malay labour, which would undertake clearing work but nothing else, and Tamil labour, which was considered essential for work in the plantation, is an interesting one. So, also, is the emphasis on road frontages and health conditions. A plantation that had no present or probable access to a road had a greatly reduced value, while malaria could make whole areas of Malaya unprofitable or impossible to plant. It is worth noting that the title to this estate was an approved grant in perpetuity from the Government of the Federated Malay States, subject to an annual quit rent, after six years, of $4 per acre. As has been said in a previous chapter, the issue was a successful one, the shares going, almost immediately, to a premium. It is interesting to note that, although the expenses of forming the company were kept to the £3,500 envisaged, underwriting and brokerage expenses amounted to no less than £4,631, which represented a considerable return for Bousteads considering how little risk was involved in those days of boom.

1911. By now the area planted to rubber had almost trebled at 1,400 acres and 300 acres had been planted to coconuts. Five hundred acres had been prepared for planting, leaving only 700 acres uncleared. This was rapid progress and nine new sets of Coolie lines had to be built to accommodate the enlarged labour force.

A considerable amount of work has been done on the estate in the way of drainage and the making of roads and paths, and the whole Estate is being laid out so as to admit of good and close management and convenient working. Tapping of some of the older trees will commence before long and the estimate for rubber in 1912 is a crop of 23,000 lbs.

1912. The planted area now amounted to 2,583 acres, with all the remaining land either ready or being prepared for planting. All plantings were, as usual, interplanted with coffee, some of which had been harvested and sold locally as there was a good local Chinese demand. The decision to plant a full 1,000 acres of coconuts had been taken and a rubber factory large enough to deal with the crop from 500 acres of mature rubber had been built and equipped. However,

in view of the many improvements now being made in the methods of Rubber preparation and manufacture, the Directors have considered it best to provide factory accommodation in the meanwhile, sufficient only for the Rubber which is now coming into bearing, and to defer extensions to factory buildings and plant until the considerable acreage, planted since the Company acquired the property, approaches the bearing stage. The Directors regret to report that . . . Mr John Gibson was taken ill and had to return to England . . . They are, however, pleased to say that . . . he is making a good recovery and hopes to be able, after a few months, to return to the Federated Malay States. Mr Eric Macfadyen, a considerable Shareholder in the Company, and well known as a visiting agent . . . has joined the Board . . . and has, in Mr Gibson's absence, taken over the duties of Managing Director . . . Mr Macfadyen in his report states: 'By the extent of the work carried out here in the last two years, without anything else, the achievement which Messrs Gibson and Grieg can boast of here is quite without parallel in my experience. To a planter, however, it is made much more astonishing by the quality of the work performed.'

1913. The Directors are pleased to report that an application made more than a year ago for an additional block of 1000 acres of excellent land, adjoining the Company's Estate has recently been approved by the Government, and the grant is made on the usual terms. One hundred and seventy-two acres of this new land have already been felled, burned and cleared and are now being planted in coconuts. The Estate has been visited by Mr Quartley who states in his report:- 'A considerable area of the rubber is showing about the best growth I have ever seen . . . tapping has been well and cheaply done . . . I was very much pleased with this property, and I have no hesitation in saying that it should be one of the best estates in Selangor . . . I should like to record that it has been opened on the latest and most up-to-date lines and I congratulate the Manager on the success he has achieved.' . . .

Douglas Money, 1913.

The Profit and Loss Account shows £2391 11s. 10d. profit on the working for the year . . . The crop of Rubber amounted to 24,458 lbs. which averaged a nett average price . . . of 3s. 0.48d. per lb. The cost of production was 1s. 5.09d. per lb. The Coffee crop harvested amounted to 6,180 tins of cherry which were sold locally for £510 14s. 9d. . . . Owing to the fact that the area brought under cultivation has considerably exceeded the original programme, further Capital will be required . . . Notice is given of a Resolution to be submitted to an Extraordinary General Meeting to increase the Nominal Capital of the Company to £150,000 . . . The Directors propose to create £35,000 of 7 per cent First Mortgage Convertible Debentures . . . This issue of Debentures will not be underwritten and it is proposed to offer them to Shareholders pro rata . . .

1914. 180 acres of the new block of 1,000 acres has been planted in rubber . . . it had been intended to plant this in coconuts . . . but the Visiting Agent . . . formed the opinion that it was better adapted for rubber . . . It has been decided for the present not to undertake any further extensions of cultivations . . . Tamil labour has increased beyond the requirements of the Estate. Steps were accordingly taken to reduce the same. There is now a labour force ample for all requirements, and the health of the coolies continues to be excellent . . . The crop of rubber . . . amounted to 63,482 lbs against the estimate of 60,000 lbs . . . The first Latex portion . . . was prepared in the form of Smoked Sheet . . . The all-in cost of production amounted to 1s. 3.34d. . . . the average gross price was 2s. 2.83d. . . . The crop of Coffee . . . amounted to 2,003 tins . . . and realised £221 0s. 2d. Owing to the rapid growth of the rubber the cutting out of the coffee interplanted in the same has been continued . . . The Profit and Loss Account shows a balance of £2,640 9s. 8d. . . . which would have justified the payment of a dividend of four per cent . . . The Directors, however, consider that in the somewhat uncertain state of affairs brought about by the war, it would be more prudent to carry this balance forward and not, for the moment, declare a dividend . . . the rates for freight and insurance against war risks are bound to fluctuate . . .

1915. The Government of the Federated Malay States has now formally approved of the Company's application for a reduction of the quit rent on the whole of its property . . . Arrangements have been made to considerably extend the factory for dealing with the now rapidly increasing crop of rubber, and the necessary machinery has been ordered, but owing to the War the delivery of the same has been considerably delayed . . . The average price realised for the rubber crop was 2s. 2.54d. . . . the all-in cost of production was 11.26d. . . . Nearly all of the coffee has now been eradicated and there will not, therefore, be anything from this source in the future . . . The profit on the year's working is £11,618 17s. 0d. . . . The Directors recommend a Final Dividend of five per cent, making nine per cent for the year . . .

NOTE: The world crop of plantation rubber, which amounted to 17,000 tons in 1911, had risen to 75,000 tons by 1914 and, for the first time, a continuing fall in rubber prices was experienced. There was therefore pressure on the government to reduce the standard quit rent of $4 an acre, since this was paid on all land, planted or otherwise, and had begun to represent a considerable burden on some of the newer estates. An agreement was finally reached which delayed the payment of the full quit rent until the twenty-first instead of the sixth year of the original grant. Although prices were falling, costs were as well, partly because wages had been cut but principally because, as the trees matured, tapping costs decreased. It is worth noting that by 1914 almost 900,000 acres had been planted to rubber in Malaya alone.

1916. Three hundred acres of coconut land were interplanted with rubber since 'the development of the palms on the area dealt with was not considered satisfactory', and 125 acres of new rubber land was planted. The new plant ordered for the factory had been installed and the quality of the rubber produced was now satisfactory. The rubber crop amounted to 397,000 pounds and realised 2s. 4.84d. per pound. Production costs were 1s. 1.47d. per pound as opposed to 11.26d. the previous year. 'The higher cost of production is due partly to the increased cost of freight, but mainly to a larger proportion of the crop having been obtained from young trees just commencing to bear.' Profits for the year were £27,724 15s. 1d., and a final dividend of 10 per cent, making 15 per cent in all, was paid. Seven hundred and fifty acres of adjoining land, known as the Irongray Estate were bought for £1,500 and were being cleared for planting. Since extra capital would be needed it was proposed to issue the 150,000 unissued shares. Arrangements were made to begin writing off the investment in buildings and plant and £2,000 was transferred to a reserve account.

1917. The rubber crop was 611,000 pounds, the all-in cost 1s. 2.5d. and the average gross price 2s. 7.7d. Costs of production had increased, partly because of further increases in the cost of freight and insurance and partly because of the cost of clearing away dead timber. The shortage of shipping was becoming a limiting factor, and as a consequence 'the maximum yield obtainable is not being aimed at, and this also tends to increase production costs'. The profit for the year was £47,542 18s. 9d. A total dividend for the year of 20 per cent was paid, £3,000 was written off in depreciations and £12,500 was placed in the reserve account. It is interesting to note that, in spite of the greatly increased acreage, the profits had never reached the levels predicted for them in the 1910 prospectus.

1918. There were now 3,000 acres under rubber and 750 under coconuts, the latter having produced a first crop which was sold for £813. The rubber crop was 634,551 pounds, the all-in cost 1s. 5.17d. and the average gross price 1s. 11.72d. per pound.

In conformity with the proposals of the Rubber Growers' Association this Company agreed to reduce its output for the twelve months terminating on 31 December. But for this voluntary restriction of output a larger crop would have been obtained . . . In the absence of any adequately supported scheme for restriction of output beyond December this Company will return to its normal production, except that, for the present, it is not proposed to take into tapping any new trees.

The gross profit was £21,071 4s. 6d. After depreciation of £2,500 and the transfer of £8,000 to reserve, a dividend of 10 per cent was paid.

NOTE: This is the first reference to a problem that was to continue to be of the greatest importance to the rubber plantation industry from now on – the problem of controlling and, if necessary, restricting production. Initially it appeared to be no more than a wartime shipping problem. Tonnage could not be spared for all the rubber Malaya could now produce and the Rubber Growers' Association suggested that plantations should restrict their production to 80 per cent of normal as a purely wartime gesture. There were other wartime problems as well. The United States on entering the war cut back its rubber imports by almost one third and imposed price controls. Since total car production in the United States had increased sharply due to the introduction of assembly-line techniques, the restrictions in this, the most important of all markets, threatened to bring about a complete collapse in rubber prices. Exports to Germany, another important market, had, of course, stopped, and rubber stocks were building up. On the other hand, a great post-war increase in the demand for rubber was confidently predicted and planting continued at such a rate that, by 1918, 1,307,000 acres had been planted in Malaya alone.

1920. No new areas were planted, but the adjoining Padang Rusa estate of 713 acres, 393 of these already planted to rubber, was bought for £10,145. This brought the company's total acreage up to 5,335 and led to a reorganisation of the estate which was now divided into two divisions under separate superintendents, these divisions being called Brooklands West and Brooklands East. The rubber crop was 590,612 pounds 'due to the voluntary restriction of output decided upon in view of the shortage of shipping facilities . . .'. The gross average price was 1s. 6.51d. and the f.o.b. cost 9.38d. The year's profit fell to £14,342, which allowed a dividend of 10 per cent to be paid with depreciations of only £1,000, nothing put to reserve and a greatly reduced carry-forward. The remaining unissued shares, 122,944 in number, were now issued at a premium of 2s. to provide extra capital.

The health of the Tamil Labour Force has not been as satisfactory as usual . . . The Estate suffered severely from the Influenza Epidemic . . . and instructions have been given to improve in every way the labour housing accommodation on the Estates and to carry out any other measures . . . to improve the standard of health of the Company's employees.

1921. The crisis through which the industry is passing . . . is the outcome of the excess of supply over demand . . . The Rubber Growers' Association last autumn proposed a scheme under which those who contracted to do so were to reduce their output by twenty-five per cent . . . we joined in that scheme, but events have shown that the measure of restriction has proved to be totally inadequate to remedy the position that has arisen . . . it is doubtful whether it can be said that all the members are actually producing twenty-five per cent less than their normal crop would have been . . . A proposal was made that the Government of the Federated Malay States should . . . introduce legislation . . . to restrict by law the output of rubber by something like fifty per cent . . . and that other rubber producing countries should be invited to do the same . . . This proposal has fallen through . . .

The price of rubber that year dropped to 10.5*d*. per pound, while the cost of production was 11.5*d*. There was a loss on the year's working of £2,638 2*s*. This was the last General Meeting at which Edgar Money took the chair.

1922. Douglas Money said:

I am occupying the chair today in the absence of my father . . . I am sure that you wish, as I do, that he will soon be able to return . . . The Crop was sold at a gross average price of 8.43*d*. per lb. and the all-in cost was 6.85*d*. per lb. . . . A substantial reduction was made in the cost of production . . . While the greatest economy is being observed, nothing has been done at the expense of efficient cultivation . . . One of the causes of lower costs has been the lower price of rice and lower wages. The latter items are closely allied, as cheap rice at once leads to reduced cost of all commodities. This enables the coolie to maintain his standard of living on a lower wage, and I do not wish you to think that the company has treated its labour force unfairly during the recent crisis . . . As you are probably aware, the Stevenson Committee's scheme has been adopted . . . We have every reason to be satisfied with the results . . . The price of spot rubber is now 1*s*. 2*d*. per lb., at which price our reduced output will show us a substantially larger profit than would have been possible on unrestricted production with rubber selling at about 9*d*. per lb. . . . There was no desire to push the price up to 4*s*. or 5*s*. a lb. and produce another boom. At the same time I would like to see the price rise to 1*s*. 9*d*. because at that price we can pay good dividends . . . unless rubber is kept at around 2*s*. a lb. the Americans will not extend their factories to develop new uses for rubber . . .

A profit of £7,000 was made on the year's workings, but no

dividend was paid and £16,000 was transferred to reserve, bringing that account up to £40,000. This, together with a sharp drop in working costs, demonstrates the prudence Douglas was to bring to his administration of the rubber companies, and his determination to become a low-cost producer of rubber.

NOTE: The government's decision to implement the Stevenson Committee's Report was pushed through by Churchill, then Colonial Secretary, and represented a reversal of earlier *laissez faire* attitudes. Since Malaya and Ceylon at that time produced 75 per cent of the world's plantation rubber, it was thought that the refusal of the Dutch to implement a similar scheme in the Dutch East Indies would not destroy its chances of success. The need to do something had become urgent. The Malayan government was running a deficit because of the loss of rubber revenues. Large numbers of Tamil labourers had been laid off and would have to be shipped back to India, which would mean labour shortages and an inability to work the plantations properly once world stocks had been reduced and the demand for rubber started to increase. The sale of rubber to the United States was especially important to the British economy since Britain was now heavily indebted to the United States as a result of the war. Finally, Churchill maintained that there was a debt of honour owed to Malaya because of her war efforts, which had included supplying the British Navy with a battleship, a gesture a former First Lord would find it impossible to forget. There was, moreover, a suspicion that the Americans were not unwilling to see the rubber plantation industry in difficulties since this would allow them to buy a large stake in Malayan rubber at little cost to themselves.

These were all reasons for acting, but there were political and practical difficulties to consider. Any attempt at a managed market offended the free traders, who were still a potent force in British politics. America would resent Britain's using her monopoly position in rubber to restrict supplies of one of the few raw materials that then had to be imported into the United States. The Dutch insisted that to co-operate would be against their free trade principles, quite forgetting their former spice monopolies. There was, moreover, the practical difficulty of policing any compulsory scheme so far as the smallholders in Malaya were concerned. Nearly half a million acres of rubber were grown in Malaya on native smallholdings. Where a sharp fall in prices would eventually force the rubber estates to reduce production or even stop it altogether, it would have little effect on the smallholder, who had no labour to pay, who was self-sufficient in food and who would respond to lower prices for his only cash crop by increasing rather than reducing rubber production, which he could do for a considerable period by heavier tapping. To impose production and export quotas on great numbers of smallholders was an administrative task of some complexity.

Nevertheless the attempt was made, and it succeeded. Standard production quotas were imposed and exportable quotas enforced by means of export duties fixed on a sliding scale that operated around what was considered a 'fair price' of between 1s. and 1s. 3d. per pound. For the first year, a production quota of 60 per cent was set. This soon doubled the market price. Surplus stocks began to disappear, and by 1925 the price of rubber had risen to 4s. 7d. a pound. There was strong anti-British feeling in the United States as a result, and both Ford and Firestone started large rubber plantations in regions outside British control. The exportable quota was then increased to 80 and ultimately 100 per cent, and the 'pivot price' raised to 1s. 9d. per pound. This had the effect of bringing the market price down to at least the level of the 'pivot price', and the scheme would have been considered entirely successful by consumers and producers alike had it not been for the actions of the Dutch, who greatly expanded their production in the Dutch East Indies.

Douglas Money had taken a great interest in the former attempts to control rubber production by voluntary means while he was still in Malaya, and had sent a long paper to the Hon. W. Duncan, a member of the Federal Council and head of the Duncan Committee that produced a scheme for compulsory restrictions which was never adopted. In his paper, Douglas had suggested several ingenious variations on that scheme. Now, in London, he was to become the almost official spokesman of the restrictionists.

1923. This company is fortunate in having a low capital per acre, and for that reason it is anticipated that we shall be able to earn at least ten per cent for you during the current year. It may seem a fair return for a rubber property, but in this particular company I think we are justified in looking forward to very much better dividends than ten per cent . . . Our justification for expecting

increased profits is that we have put back into the estate a considerable sum of money from our profit and loss account. The
Development Reserve account stands at £40,000. That sum, as
you are aware, has been earned by the company and put back
into the property and for that reason we are fully justified in
anticipating very much better returns than ten per cent . . . The
position of the rubber industry is not entirely satisfactory . . .
Prices have fallen below the pivot price of 1s. 3d. Under the
restriction scheme when the London price has averaged 1s. 3d.
for three months we are allowed to export an additional five per
cent of our standard allowance. That additional five per cent
might be considered welcome, but I can assure you that we
would much rather remain at sixty per cent . . .

The profit for the year was £15, 228 6s. 5d., and a dividend of 10
per cent was paid.

1925. We have acquired a further 1,300 acres of jungle . . . we were
only able to get it for oil palm cultivation and are unable to plant
rubber on it . . . The directors felt that it would not be a bad
thing to start an oil palm cultivation should rubber prove a disap-
pointment . . . The cultivation of the oil palm is in its infancy.
The trade knows it chiefly as a wild commodity, like rubber
before the plantation industry started . . . Under proper conditions a return of fifteen to twenty per cent on the capital employed may be expected . . . But it is common knowledge that in
the course of the next seven or eight years a very large area will
have to be planted in rubber in some part of the world. We are
undoubtedly the premier nation in the production of rubber and
it is inconceivable that the Malay States Government will refuse
us permission to extend our acreage . . .

The profit for the year was £43,390, and the gross average price
2s. per pound. The dividend was 20 per cent. It is interesting to
note that, restrictionist though he was, the rise in rubber prices was
tempting him to complain about the restrictions on new plantings
of rubber.

1926. A block of good jungle land adjoining the Estate has been
acquired from the government on favourable terms, and as lab-

our is abundant, extension in rubber can be carried out cheaply
... A moderate increase in the Authorised Capital is therefore
proposed ...

The profit for the year was £73,606 3s. 8d. The average price was
1s. 11.04d., the big increase in profit coming from an increase in the
standard production quota. Moreover the restrictions on new rubber plantings had been relaxed. A dividend of 40 per cent was paid.

1927. Last year ... the directors obtained a Government block of
land for the cultivation of oil palms. We had no doubt that if
rubber did not improve we should be quite pleased with a plantation of oil palms ... Prosperity did, however, return to rubber
and we succeeded in getting the Government to substitute rubber grants at a small premium. We have lost no time in cutting
out the young palms and putting in the rubber plants. I am sure
shareholders will view with mixed feelings the increased planting
of rubber and it may be difficult to justify when apparently the
world is able to produce more rubber than it can absorb. The
rubber industry, however, is different from other industries such
as cotton which have an annual crop, and it takes at least eight
years from the time you start a rubber estate before you get any
dividend. That means one must ignore the immediate outlook,
but look to the rather more distant future when, if our calculations are right, the world will require a great deal more rubber
than is in sight at the present time. You may have seen it
reported recently that Mr Henry Ford intends to develop a huge
rubber area in Brazil ... the reason for this, no doubt, is that in
the opinion of Mr Ford a great deal more rubber will be required
eight years hence ... I do not think Mr Ford has been moved by
spite against Britain ... If he is able to bring this big scheme into
being it will be because he fears that in the not distant future his
huge factories may be turning out cars for the million while the
world is unable to produce sufficient rubber for the tyres at a
price which makes motoring possible for the ordinary man.
Whether any considerable area can be developed on a commercial basis is another point ... If Brazil cannot produce rubber at,
say, 1s. 3d. a lb. Mr Henry Ford will be unsuccessful and Eastern
plantations will hold the field. On the other hand, it may be quite
possible that both areas will be required. That is the view your

Directors have taken . . . The new fields we are planting or will plant – for it is our intention to plant up the whole of our available land – will produce good crops of rubber at the lowest cost in the East.

NOTE: The net profit for the year, with an average gross price for rubber of 1s. 6.15d. was £42,649 9s. and a dividend of 25 per cent was paid. The reference to Henry Ford reflects the very real tension existing at that time between Britain and the United States over rubber. The Americans regarded the Stevenson scheme as an attempt to blackmail the Americans on behalf of a British Empire that had, in any case, to be destroyed, while the British thought that the Americans, as usual, were being anti-British and wanting to take over the British-controlled rubber industry on the cheap. Certainly it was American agitation against the Stevenson scheme that helped to bring about its collapse the following year, though the main factor was the more immediate problem of the Dutch. As the Malay government operated the system of production and export quotas, based on what were sometimes unrealistic assessments, and attempted to control the planting of new rubber, so the Dutch in the East Indies encouraged the expansion of rubber planting both on estates and smallholdings until, for the first time, the East Indies emerged as almost as large a rubber producer as Malaya. The consequences were chaos.

1928. While the results are not altogether as satisfactory as were anticipated . . . they might have been considerably worse . . . the sudden end of restrictions was due, in my opinion, to the methods of assessing estates . . . last year when exports were at sixty per cent of standard . . . a great deal more than sixty per cent was coming out of the restriction area . . . and that was due . . . to the overassessments that had taken place. That was the reason for the agitation that broke out . . . for the abolition of restriction . . . I cannot take a pessimistic view of rubber . . . Within the next few years . . . supply and demand should balance within about five per cent, but whether it will be five per cent over-production or five per cent over-consumption one cannot say . . . if the over-production is within five per cent prices should remain at 9d., but if there is five per cent under-production then we may see 1s. rubber . . . The fact that an overall average yield from the estate of 400 lbs. an acre can be obtained at an all-in cost of just over $5\frac{1}{2}d$. a lb. shows that the management of the estate is first class.

The profit was £18,949, and the dividend of 10 per cent took almost all of it, but –

> The balance sheet shows a strong cash position, there being £27,000 in War Loans and £20,000 in the Bank. That shows that we should safely get through a long period of slump, but shareholders should not consider that present conditions are necessarily slump conditions . . .

Douglas Money (right) at Bruce Money's wedding, 1929. Alice Money (left) (Douglas's mother) wearing bead necklace.

1929. In the Directors' Report no details are given as to cost of production or sale price. That is the general practice now adopted by rubber companies . . . Needless to say we should be pleased to boast of our extremely low costs, but the shareholders can find that out for themselves by a simple sum of arithmetic . . .

I do not want to deal at this meeting with the question of bud grafting . . . we do, however, have to look a long way forward, and the only way the rubber industry can protect itself from the huge increase in output, expected by the adoption of bud grafting, is by trying to find new uses for rubber and extending existing uses . . . Nothing so far has turned up which has added substantially to the consumption of rubber. I myself have spent a good deal of time on this work, and I know the difficulties involved . . . I will give just one instance, rubber flooring. You will see a beautiful one in this room and there are no doubt thousands where they can be afforded, but you can take it from me that the whole of the rubber flooring turned out in the world . . . has not helped the rubber industry by so much as one eighth of a penny per lb. . . . The only hope is to develop a rubber flooring that will compete with medium priced linoleum . . . There is no doubt that the industry depends for its existence on the increased use of the motor vehicle . . . It might be possible by means of propaganda to discourage the use of horses in the streets of big towns. Traffic is extremely slow, chiefly due to the antiquated means of transport. The horse, however, stands in a peculiar position. Known as a 'noble animal' its 'nobility' is respected and I think it is what I might call the horse snob who is responsible to a great extent for the retention of that animal on the roads . . . We have to look for a greatly extended use of rubber if, in the years to come . . . this industry is to remain a big British industry and not to develop into a native industry where the commodity price is only a fraction above the cost of production. You have to face the potent fact that if bud grafted rubber will give the big yields that are expected of it consumption must increase very considerably . . . We have purchased the best budding material we can get and the manager is experimenting with the method on a considerable scale . . . We have a great deal of jungle still uncultivated . . . which is suitable for planting rubber. This will only be opened up when the science has become more exact. The clearings planted in 1927, 1928 and 1929 will be wholly or partially budded, but I prefer to regard this work as experimental . . .

The profit was £34,327 7s. 11d., and the dividend paid was 15 per cent.

NOTE: This is the first reference to bud grafting, a new technique, evolved in the Dutch East Indies, for producing high-yielding rubber trees. It was the first of those many advances in rubber growing that were to push yields per acre up from around 400 pounds to around 2,000 pounds. Douglas was quick to grasp the implications of bud grafting, for it meant that methods of controlling production and stimulating consumption had to be found. He was to spend an increasing amount of time investigating new uses for rubber and was, at various times, to believe that he may have found an answer in rubber roads, rubber car springs, rubber upholstery, rubber mattresses and rubber floor coverings. Yet, as his remarks about 'the noble animal' reveal, there was always something of the White Knight in him, albeit a White Knight with the zeal of a prophet.

1930. In spite of what had been said the year before, figures for cost and price were revealed. Cost was 5.28*d*. per pound and average price was 6.69*d*. per pound. The net profit was £8,776 17s. 7*d*., which was added to reserve. No dividend was paid.

1931. The cost was recorded as 3.02*d*. per pound, and the price as 3.09*d*. per pound. The profit was £1,693 11s. 4*d*. No dividend was paid.

1932. The cost was 2.17*d*. per pound, and the price 2.07*d*. per pound. There was a loss of £1,000 on the year's working and no dividend was paid.

1933. The cost was 1.66*d*. per pound, and the price 2.18*d*. per pound. The profit was £3,011 12s. No dividend was paid.

1934. The cost was 2.25*d*. per pound, and the price 4.12*d*. per pound. The net profit was £9,754 13s. 10*d*., and a dividend of 5 per cent was paid. For the first time in four years, the company published a report of its meeting. The year before Douglas had said:

> What I have said just now are the kind of remarks I should like to see appear in the press, but I do not think we shall publish any report of this meeting, as I do not think that the Company is justified in so using its funds.

This year in which the report was published marked the end of the acute phase of the rubber crisis that lasted from the winding up of the Stevenson scheme to the introduction of a new international rubber restriction scheme, to which Britain, Holland, France and Belgium – i.e. all the rubber producing countries – subscribed.

New planting and replanting were forbidden and production in all the countries was scaled down. Every producer was issued with coupons specifying the quantity of rubber he could produce.

1935. Under the international scheme, the 'Standard Production' allotted for the year was 1,782,034 pounds. A net profit of £8,907 19s. 1d. was made and a dividend of 5 per cent was paid.

> I believe that the Restriction Scheme . . . will be with us for many years to come . . . I daresay all of us feel there is something uneconomic in restriction and destruction. But the Americans have come to it . . . they plough up cotton already planted, they destroy wheat and coffee and kill pigs and so on. It is unpleasant . . . and is probably the strongest indictment of the Capitalist system which has yet been made. The alternative is Communism, and I do not think any of us would like that . . .

1936. The net profit was £13,551 6s. 11d., and a dividend of 7½ per cent was paid. Douglas opened up a subject that was to concern him for some time to come, Germany's determination, under Schacht's autarchic control of her economy, to develop her Buna rubber industry and stop buying natural rubber:

> It has been reported that German manufacturers of motor cars have their factories full of cars which they are unable to deliver because they have no tyres to put them on, and that that is due to the shortage of crude rubber, and further that such shortage is due to lack of exchange . . . I was interested in this, and so I took the trouble to telephone various senior officials at the Board of Trade and ask for information . . . I was told they had no further information and that it was not for the Board to make any suggestion . . . as it was purely a matter for the rubber growers themselves . . . It did occur to me that something should be done in the way of offering rubber to Germany on credit . . . It is a matter of some urgency, as we do not want to encourage the production of synthetics . . . It must be remembered that we are working the Rubber Restriction Scheme for the benefit of the whole world, but at the same time Germany has every right to say that we are boosting up the price by restricting output and that they are going short because they cannot afford to buy it. It is no good our saying that they ought not to be short of money and that they would not be short of money if they did not spend

so much on armaments. I am not quite sure that this expenditure
of theirs on armaments will not be to our ultimate benefit . . .

Douglas then entered into very active negotiations with any officials or trade associations, British or German, he thought he could
interest in his ideas. It all ended, almost a year later, with a message
transmitted to him from the Reichsstelle für Devisenbewirtschaftung
in Berlin, which ran:

> I am instructed to inform you that for the time being we do not
> wish to consider seriously the plan for importing rubber on
> credit . . .

1937. The net profit was £24,408 14s. and the dividend paid was
12½ per cent.
1938. The profit was £19,786 9s. 3d., and a dividend of 5 per cent
was paid.

> You may perhaps be surprised at the Board's decision to re-
> duce the dividend to five per cent. We could . . . had we thought fit
> to do so, have recommended a dividend of ten per cent . . . and
> we should have given you that had the International Rubber
> Regulation Committee acted differently . . . Although I have no
> desire to criticise any members of the Committee, I feel that the
> Committee as a whole deserves very severe criticism . . . at their
> meeting this month they were obviously actuated by two
> motives. One was to appease the American manufacturers. This
> country seems to go round the world appeasing everybody and
> satisfying no one . . .

1939. The net profit was £21,817 3s. 7d., and a dividend of 9 per
cent was paid.
Douglas had for many years conducted what could be described
as guerrilla warfare against the then mighty Dunlop Rubber
Company. He did this because he thought it wrong for rubber
manufacturers to become rubber planters on such a large scale as to
be able to exert a decisive influence as producers when, in fact, they
were truly processors. As processors, they wanted cheap rubber
and no restrictions, and they used their votes as planters to that
effect. Douglas's was the familiar complaint farmers make against
the great agri-businesses that may or may not be organised ver-

tically. To carry on his sporadic warfare, he bought one Dunlop share. This allowed him to attend Dunlop's Annual General Meeting in order to harass the chairman and present what he considered to be the planter's authentic viewpoint. He was not always successful. After one such intervention in 1934, the chairman, in reply, said:

'Mr Money has stated quite frankly that he represents the plantation side of the industry. I wonder whether he will be equally frank as to the size of his interest in the Dunlop Company' . . . he paused to give Mr Money an opportunity to reply. Mr Money did not answer . . . 'Then Mr Money has raised the question of the price level at which the Board thought rubber should be held. I do not think it prudent to give an answer . . . but I gather that Mr Money, as Chairman of the Kampong Kuantan Company published a statement that said:- "The European countries that owe money to America could pay off the debt by so restricting supplies of rubber that the Americans would be forced to pay up to five shillings a pound for that essential commodity" (Laughter) He could not agree . . . that rubber at five shillings a pound would be in the interests of the Dunlop Rubber Company . . .'

Douglas may have been defeated on that occasion, but he remained decidedly unbowed. A few years later he was to comment:

Before I close my remarks I would like to refer to the question of manufacturers owning rubber plantations . . . I feel . . . they have gone far enough into the business of growing their own rubber and would be well advised not to carry that side of their business any further. If they do there will always be the possibility that the plantations will take a hand in the manufacturing game . . . A co-operative factory, either in the East or in England, financed by the plantation companies, could produce motor car tyres of first-class quality, fully equal to those produced by old-established manufacturers at a cost which would certainly not exceed thirty per cent of the present retail price of tyres . . . This would certainly jeopardise the position of all big manufacturers in this country, and I wish to make it perfectly clear that the plantation owners are not ignorant of the true facts of the case . . .

1940. The net profit was £47,207 5s. 8d. The dividend paid was 12½ per cent. The chairman's report was not published.

1941. The profit for the year was £50,035 6s. 8d. An interim dividend of 5 per cent was paid, but no final dividend. £36,000 was set aside as provision for taxation as against £23,000 the previous year, and a balance of £18,502 2s. 9d. was carried forward. Once again the chairman's report was not published. The war was beginning to bite and Douglas acted with his customary prudence by husbanding his resources.

1942. The accounts and report were, in accordance with wartime economy measures, printed on a small flysheet. The profit was £22,502 2s. 8d., which included a reserve for loss on realisation of excess stocks that was no longer required of £4,000. In a bald statement, the chairman said:

> The Company's property is situated in the State of Selangor . . . which territory has been occupied by the enemy. Members should note that the Federated Malay States are, or rather were, a Protectorate and not a Colony or Dominion. The defence of Malaya was accordingly reserved by the Imperial Government, and as circumstances made it expedient to divert arms and equipment required for the defence of Malaya to other Fronts, it is clear that owners of property in Malaya are entitled to fair compensation, preferably by remission of all claims to taxes that are outstanding . . . As the future of the Company depends chiefly upon the good-will and just dealings of H. M. Government, it would be premature for the Directors to recommend voluntary liquidation or other steps which might be in the best interests of the Members . . . Official news has been received that the Company's Manager, Mr P. C. Fisher, is a prisoner of war. Of his Assistants, Mr C. Grant was able to get away to South Africa, but no official news has been received of Messrs A. Koford and H. D. Quartley, and they are presumed to be prisoners of war . . .

1944. A loss of £1,390 6s. 6d., which represented the London office expenses, was reported.

> The Company's Estates remain in enemy occupation and no news of their condition has been received . . . After long negotiations with the Inland Revenue Authorities agreement was reached resulting in a substantial reduction of the liability for

taxation. Under this arrangement the amount payable by the Company should not exceed £35,000 unless a resumption of profitable trading is possible after the defeat of the Japanese . . . Regarding our Assistants, Messrs A. Koford and H. D. Quartley, there is still no news . . .

1945. There was a profit, how earned is not explained, of £121 18s. 3d.

The Company's Estates remain in enemy occupation and no news of their condition has been received. No official news of their condition has been received. No official news has yet been received regarding the Estate Assistants, Messrs A. Koford and H. D. Quartley . . .

1946. This was the last of the greatly reduced wartime accounts. It had been extended to a double sheet. All the wartime reports were addressed as from 8 Clifton Road, Wimbledon, instead of from what had been the company offices at Walsingham House, Seething Lane.

A profit on £412 9s. 5d. was reported, being the balance left from interest on investments after meeting London office expenses.

A short report has been received from a member of the Inspection Party which, under Government auspices, has toured Malaya with a view to passing on to proprietors an early report on conditions. Generally speaking the Estate has not been badly damaged by the Japanese, although certain buildings, plant and equipment have been looted or requisitioned. Rehabilitation will cost a considerable sum and the Directors will claim damages from H. M. Government, although collection . . . may take a long time to achieve . . . It is anticipated that production of rubber on a reduced scale will begin at an early date. Up to now H. M. Government has not seen fit to pay the Company for rubber which has been requisitioned, and the price paid for current production in Malaya is estimated to be well under the cost of production . . . The Government Departments concerned are being reverently approached by the Rubber Growers' Association with a view to receiving more charity, and sharehol- ders must patiently wait for results . . . It will be remembered that in the Accounts of 1942 the estimated value of Liquid Assets in Malaya at date of enemy occupation were written off. So far no information regarding same has been received . . . It is with very much regret that we must report the death, whilst a prisoner of war in Burma, of Mr Douglas Quartley . . . he made a most gallant escape from Singapore but was ultimately made a prisoner in Sumatra, whence he was taken by the Japanese to Burma . . . Mr P. C. Fisher, the Manager of Brooklands, survived the horrors of imprisonment and work on the Siam-Burma Railway, and we are glad to say that he is making a complete recovery and hopes to return to Brooklands this Spring . . . Many members of the Asiatic staff survived the Japanese occupation, and there were doubtless many instances of devoted service on the Estate where the Japanese forced the Staff and labour to work the property under difficult and unpleasant conditions . . .

There followed a chairman's statement, in which Douglas said, among other things:

Under the Scheme approved by the Colonial Office, companies were obliged to join groups of not less than 100,000 acres of rubber for the purpose of pooling supplies etc. This company joined the Harrisons and Crosfield Group . . . Much has been written about the unsatisfactory price which H. M. Government are at present paying for rubber now being produced . . . It would appear that the Authorities wish to provoke the Industry into taking strike action . . . Apparently the Ministry of Supply find no difficulty in agreeing to pay rubber manufacturing companies in England for tyres and equipment prices which have allowed those companies to earn colossal profits far in excess of those earned before the war. It is a little difficult to understand why a Ministry which is prepared to guarantee excessive profits to consumers of plantation rubber should refuse to pay even cost price for the raw material which they requisition from a poverty stricken community, both of smallholders and shareholders in Plantation Companies . . . I asked the Chairman of the Dunlop Rubber Company at his annual meeting who fixed the price paid for his tyres and other goods sold to the Ministry of Supply. An evasive answer revealed that the Company had come to an agreement with the Ministry on prices, and one can only assume that when the Company's swollen profits were finally disclosed, steps were taken to arrange for a reduction in prices which could reduce the Company's profits to those current before the war . . .

In the past, the Ministry of Supply have employed prominent ex-employees of Dunlops to regulate the supply of raw rubber . . . Today, it is probable that the Ministry is guided by Civil Servants who have had no experience whatsoever of the commercial production of plantation rubber . . . The reaction of producers may or may not be urgently brought home to those bureaucratic inhabitants of Whitehall . . .

Concentrated Latex Factory, 1947. Note pulleys and belts driving centrifuges on the left, which are used to concentrate the field latex prior to preservation and shipment in liquid form throughout the world.

1947. A loss of £6,478 0s. 3d. was made.

Information has been received from Messrs Harrisons and Crosfields Ltd that a profit of approximately one farthing a pound was made by the sub-group to which this Company belongs on Working Account. This profit, apparently meagre, may be accounted for by reason of the inclusion of charges for Rehabilitation which would normally have been debited to Capital Account . . . Very good progress has been made . . . with the reorganisation of the Estate. High yields are being obtained from a comparatively large area of budded rubber, and this is helping to keep down working costs . . . Shortly before the Japanese occupation the Company had started to ship concentrated rubber latex which met with a ready sale at profitable prices. About two years ago additional centrifuges were ordered for the Manufacturers and these have been installed and are about to produce latex for which there is a very large demand . . .

1948. The Profit on Working for the year was £23,028 16s. 0d. but after charging Rehabilitation Expenditure £14,277 1s. 3d. and Provision for Tax £3,500 and crediting Provisions no longer required and Current Assets in Malaya in 1942 recovered, amounting to £20,376 16s. 4d. there remains a credit balance of £25,628 11s. 9d. This added to the balance brought forward makes a total credit balance of £40,522 13s. 6d. which the Board proposes to carry forward – All revenue expenditure and proceeds were pooled with other members of the Harrisons and Crosfield sub-group up to 30th September 1946 . . .

1949. The profit after tax was £11,302 and a dividend of 5 per cent was paid, the first for over eight years.

At long last I am in a position to start my address without apologising to the shareholders for the absence of a dividend . . . My only regret is that it is the meagre one of five per cent. Some people might say that five per cent is good enough, but in the case of tropical agriculture it is a totally inadequate dividend. We must look for something much better than that if tropical agriculture is to be continued, and if tropical agriculture is not to be continued on a commercial basis it means that the Empire, which has already diminished very considerably and looks like diminishing still further, will have to be wound up completely . . . You do not want me to talk about the bandits and communists and the difficulties in that direction . . . The manager and staff have to put up with very unpleasant periods and their courage and determination to carry on deserve the highest praise . . . where are the future planters to come from? There are not the number of people in England, or even in Scotland today that are needed to develop tropical agriculture adequately. I have tried and other companies have tried to get youngsters to go out to Malaya and take up rubber planting, but you just cannot get them – not of the right type. I could get hundreds of people to go out tomorrow

– people with good records – but they would not make planters. A planter has to be a very specialised individual, and just cannot be picked up by the dozen. That is half the trouble of course so far as the ground nut scheme is concerned. Do not think I do not approve of the scheme to grow ground nuts. My only criticism is that it was on too large a scale to start with . . . instead of talking about millions of acres they should have said – 'We are going to try 50,000 acres and see how we get on with that.' That would have been much wiser, but instead of doing that, they started on a vast scale, bought a lot of obsolete machinery and sent out unsuitable individuals to work it. It would have been better if the Government, instead of throwing millions into Africa in the useless attempt to grow ground nuts commercially . . . had given a subsidy to the rubber plantations to cut out their poor yielding rubber and substitute an equivalent acreage of oil palms . . . It is unlikely . . . that the world is going to suffer from an over-production of oil seeds in the next twenty years . . . That, of course, sounds ridiculous when we know that there was a big over-production of oil seeds in the '30s, but let us give credit where it is due. This is not a political meeting and I do not wish to be political, but the exponents of the Labour policy say that the reason . . . was that the economic system throughout the world prevented the poor from getting the nourishment they needed. One has to admit that there is an element of truth in that; there were vast numbers of people who would have bought twice as much margarine if they could have afforded it. As things have developed throughout the world – wages have increased, especially amongst the poor – the demand for oil seeds will be very much greater for years to come.

1950. The gross profit was £32,338, and a dividend of 10 per cent was paid.

Shareholders will doubtless have been very agreeably surprised by the very great improvement that has recently taken place in the Industry . . . the change was not due to any improvement in rubber prices following devaluation . . . Last year I forecast a heavy demand for our latex within a reasonable period . . . at the present time latex from a well tested and reliable source can be sold readily at a remunerative price . . . We are selling our latex all over the world, and it is clear that considerable goodwill is being built up as users have found that Brooklands latex has properties which make it easy to process during foam manufacture. In the United States they are now willing to embark on latex foam manufacture for cushioning in spite of the fact that latex is costing far more than it did when they protested that the price was too high to make business possible on a commercial scale . . . Last year I referred to a proposal that the British Government should finance . . . the conversion of obsolete rubber into Oil Palm plantations. In due course I communicated with the Secretary of State for the Colonies . . . The subsequent history of these negotiations has followed the usual course and it would be too much to expect any enthusiasm . . .

Shareholders who have studied the Balance Sheet will realise that the Company has been handicapped to some extent by a shortage of working capital. This deficiency would not have occurred had the Government of Malaya made any serious effort to meet the just claims for War Damage of this and other Rubber Plantation Companies owning estates in the Peninsula . . . I have repeatedly denounced the same Government for this and other shortcomings . . . The Plantation Industry has shown outstanding weakness in its approach to such matters, and it has been too easy for the Colonial Office and the local administration to 'pass the buck' to each other when any uncomfortable questions are asked. In the result it has been found possible to treat not only the Rubber and Tin Industries, but also vast numbers of permanent residents with studied indifference and complete lack of humanity . . .

It is not surprising therefore that public opinion in this country has demonstrated clearly that Malaya is not expected to survive as a British Protectorate . . . Almost daily there are reports of . . . murderous attacks by bandits who appear to be able to hold their own successfully against a huge army of soldiers and police . . . Banditry in Malaya is, of course, only partially due to the policy of Communist Governments. The Chinese have for centuries suffered from the activities of bandits . . . In China, this regrettable activity was borne by the nation with a patient shrug as they realised that taxation of some kind would always be inflicted on the ordinary citizen, and that the collections made by the bandits were on the whole modest in comparison with the taxes legally levied in other countries by respectable Governments. When the

British Authorities were permitted to return to Malaya as a result of the dropping of two atom bombs on Japan, rubber producers were forced to sell their hard won post-war crops to the Authorities for the miserable price of ten pence per lb. At that time the same Authorities were paying Ceylon producers one shilling and sixpence per lb. . . . although that fortunate island had escaped invasion . . . Political folly of this kind and the lack of imagination that failed to handle the anti-Japanese army remnants tactfully, encouraged the profession of banditry and the Communists soon saw their opportunity for providing leadership and training in Communist principles. Warnings by resident planters, miners and merchants fell unheeded on the ears of stupid officials, with the result that organised underground armies, Communist led, were enabled to harass the countryside with results which are now well known . . . It is a curious feature of our political system that responsibility for the follies I have indicated above can only be traced with great difficulty. So far, I have been unable to find out who was responsible for fixing the price of rubber at ten pence a pound at the time of the reoccupation of Malaya. The Rubber Growers' Association which should have protected the interests of its members has played a pitiful part in recent years, and has failed miserably in its duty to subscribers who have no other collective means for voicing their complaints . . .

If they had no collective means, they certainly had in Douglas Money a powerful and unceasing voice crying from the wilderness on their behalf.

1951. The profit was £82,802, and the dividend for the year was 35 per cent.

Shareholders who have now waited for many years for a reasonable return on their investment will have been gratified to see that record profits were earned for the year ended June 1951 . . . Unfortunately, during the Autumn of 1951, the Company suffered a severe drop in crop owing to Government orders prohibiting the normal running of our estates on the far side of the Langat River . . . It is obvious that no Company can produce at a reasonable cost per lb. when a crop shortage of this nature, coupled with the extra expenditure on moving Labour from one Division to another, increases the burden of General Charges . . .

Today a letter has been received from the Company's Manager in Malaya which, for the first time, holds out some hope of an improvement in the situation . . . Shareholders should realise how heavy is the burden of taxation imposed by the Malayan and British Governments on Rubber Plantation Companies . . . A total of £210,366, equivalent to one shilling and sevenpence per lb. on the crop we harvested, had to be provided against this . . . In the circumstances I cannot help recalling the words of a venerable Chinese citizen of Peking, who, when asked why his people tolerated warlords and bandits, replied that he had heard that in Great Britain there was a very powerful bandit called the Chancellor of the Exchequer, who, it was believed, took far more from the rich than any bandit in China would have deemed possible or even desirable.

1952. The gross profit for the year was £281,723, from which £156,000 had to be provided for taxation. A dividend of 35 per cent was paid.

Banditry is still causing much anxiety on the Company's properties, and the Directors regret to report that in addition to the death of Mr John Shaw and the wounding of Mr N. A. Symons . . . there were further incidents during the latter part of the year. These unfortunately resulted in the death of three members of the Asian staff and the destruction by the terrorists of a number of buildings including the contents therein . . . The buildings were covered by insurance and payment has now been received . . . A year ago I referred to the Company's claim for payment in respect of rubber commonly known as 'Booty' rubber by Government Departments in Whitehall. I regret that as the Company has now been forced to institute legal proceedings against her Majesty's Government, comment of any kind cannot be made while the matter is *sub judice* . . . The Plantation Industry remains, as before, at the mercy of the politicians in the United States, where legislation concerning synthetic rubber production and sale has determined the price of Plantation rubber in the free markets of the world. Exceptionally, Ceylon has been driven by the American politicians into trading with China, which country is glad to pay a premium of 7*d*. per lb. to secure supplies of Plantation rubber. It is now learned that the Government of Burma is arranging to ship rubber to China . . .

Criticism of American policy in the Rubber field does not mean that a poor view need be taken of President Eisenhower and his Cabinet. The administration is forced to make concessions to certain politicians, who are notoriously anti-British, and who care little, apparently, for such difficulties as may arise in the Far East and elsewhere as a result of their activities . . . In the past I have warned Shareholders that sooner or later synthetic rubber would lead to the Plantation Industry becoming largely unprofitable. The 1950–51 boom, due solely to the Korean War and American stock piling could not have been anticipated and . . . any temporary profit made by the Industry during that period will be more than lost over a period of years, through the fantastic wage increases and the high cost of living, brought about by Government spending and emergency regulations which have cost the rubber planters millions of dollars in obeying resettlement orders . . .

1953. The net profit for the year after tax was £51,265, and the dividend paid was 20 per cent.

Shareholders will doubtless be well satisfied with dividends amounting to twenty per cent in respect of a year for which many old-established Plantation Companies have been unable to pay any dividend whatsoever to their long-suffering Shareholders . . . Your Company owns Estates in an area where bandit infestation has become serious, and where Liew Kon Kim, known as 'The Bearded One', was killed by a patrol of the Suffolk Regiment. During the operations which resulted in the death of this most important leader of the insurgents we were not permitted to harvest any rubber from a large area of mature rubber. Fortunately reports from Malaya indicate a slow but steady improvement in Government control of the country. The insurgents are finding it harder to live in the jungle as gradually the Authorities have kept food supplies behind barbed wire . . . Final victory can only be won if the community is able to put its trust in Government officials and the police. Contentment in the long run can only be attained if a reasonable price is obtainable for Rubber and Tin. If over-production of rubber leads to a low price and ultimately to unemployment and low wages, it seems fantastic that the Malayan Government, through the War Damage Commission, is forcing the planting of unwanted rubber upon Companies which do not wish to plant rubber but which are unwilling to renounce their legitimate claims to compensation for rubber cut out or ruined by the Japanese invaders . . .

The drastic fall in the price of rubber . . . indicates clearly that contrary to promises given in good faith, the rulers of the United States have been unable to prevent their Government-owned synthetic rubber industry from dealing a staggering blow to all producers of Plantation rubber, with the exception of those who are prepared to sell rubber to Police State countries in defiance of wishes expressed by the U.S. authorities . . . Recently an Advisory Committee representing all countries interested in the production and consumption of rubber has been holding one of its rather pathetic sessions in London, and it may be assumed that there will be another brief communiqué informing the Public – and incidentally Rubber Shareholders – that over-production of rubber cannot be cured by any known method . . . In the past I have been a somewhat rabid advocate of schemes designed to limit the quantity of rubber destined to reach consuming centres. In those days Governments in the Far East were in full control of the countries they administered. Today the reverse is the case, and Restriction under Government control would be likely to prove useless and positively dangerous to the Industry . . .

1954. The profit after tax was £33,486, and the dividend paid was 10 per cent. The Bukit Tunggu estate of some 1,300 acres, almost all planted with mature rubber, was bought for £26,000.

The Company has completed a successful association with a small organisation producing foam rubber toys. Your Directors would gladly join with others in developing other foam rubber products which could absorb a much larger weight of rubber latex, and it is hoped that the future may show that it is not always unprofitable for producers to take a financial interest in the manufacturing side of the Industry. The Dunlop Rubber Company, a manufacturing firm, has made an outstanding success of the growing of plantation rubber in Malaya, and there seems no reason why, given suitable management, plantation companies should not embark upon foam manufacture, provided that they start operations on a small scale, and allow larger developments to follow if success rewards modest beginnings . . .

1955. The profit after tax was £55,980, and a dividend of 35 per cent was paid. As a result of the strong cash position of the company, a special distribution of 6d. per unit was also paid. The Company's War Damage claim was finally agreed at £38,490, of which £28,098 had been received.

The Accounts take no credit for the 117,026 lbs of the Company's rubber which were seized in 1945 by emissaries of the British Government and in respect of which litigation has been proceeding for several years following a number of years of fruitless negotiation . . . £3,918 has been received from Her Majesty's Government, plus all costs of the action in the High Court and Solicitor's charges. The claim was settled out of Court before trial of action, in circumstances which reflect no credit upon the Government Department concerned and their legal advisers . . .

1956. The profit after tax was £43,287, and the dividend paid was one of 50 per cent.

Your Directors have decided that a generous dividend policy is justified in view of the financial strength of your Company, and having regard to the sustained high rate of profit, due to several factors, apart from the relatively satisfactory price of the commodity . . . Out of a combined planted area of 6,860 acres, there are now 3,525 acres of Mature Clonal Rubber and 1,500 acres of young rubber . . . An opportunity has occurred for the purchase of a small estate in the Kuala Selangor District at a price which your Board consider advantageous . . . It is now very difficult to procure good rubber lands in Malaya, especially in districts where the labour is settled and where the climate is good . . .

Malaya will receive a large measure of Home Rule next year, and it is generally anticipated that wise statesmanship will avoid the errors which have unfortunately marred the records in other Eastern countries where, in accordance with Britain's declared policies, all Colonies and Protectorates were promised political freedom which was to be granted as soon as the Mother country felt it was safe to abandon the guidance which was necessary in early years . . . I would like to express my personal belief in the good sense and integrity of Tengku Abdul Rahman and those ministers who will, under his guidance, inaugurate the new era in Malaya . . .

Colonial Office rule, though on the whole benevolent, worked very much better before 1941. Since the capitulation of the Japanese in 1945, Malayan officials have on many occasions exhibited an attitude towards the rubber and tin companies which failed to appreciate how dependent the prosperity of the country was on the encouragement of capital investment in a young and underdeveloped region. It has, of course, been difficult for the ordinary citizen to find out whether blunders of administration were due to the incompetence of officials in Malaya or to inept interference by the Colonial Office . . .

1957. Profit after tax was £57,936, and a dividend of 40 per cent was paid. The company's capital was increased from £200,000 to £262,000 on ordinary stock, and £52,500 of preference stock was issued. Capital reserve was shown as having increased from £13,342 to £104,168, development reserve from £74,540 to £91,698, and general reserve from £33,500 to £87,500. The Lambourn estate of 692 acres was purchased, giving the company a total acreage of 7,931½ acres, of which 6,002 acres was in mature rubber and 1,591 in young rubber.

During the current year Malaya has achieved the status of an independent country within the Commonwealth, and it is satisfactory to know that the transition has been effected with the utmost goodwill on both sides. Politically the country shows no inclination to favour a Communist system of government, but any serious attempt by the United States or other countries in the West to displace plantation rubber in favour of synthetic substitutes could bring about great difficulties for the Rulers of Malaya, and in that case the Communist countries would lose no time in offering their assistance in return for favours which can best be left to the imagination . . .

1958. Profit after tax was £57,500, and a dividend of 30 per cent was paid. The company's authorised capital was increased from £315,000 to £565,000.

For some years now there has been a remarkable balance between the production of plantation rubber, which is quite outside anything but price control, and world consumption. Credit must be given to the Government of the United States which could wreck the plantation industry by imposing a duty on raw rubber, and by unloading strategic stocks. Competition between plantation rubber and the synthetic product has so far done no harm to either, and growers have no wish to see a rise in the price of plantation sheet rubber above 33 cents gold, at which level the world price seems to satisfy all manufacturers . . .

You will see that your Directors recommend an increase of capital . . . From time to time your Board have received proposals that they should consider the purchase of other estates in Malaya, and as you are aware this policy has been followed in the past, with the result that the Company's acreage has been increased substantially, particularly by the issue of shares in part consideration and partly out of the Company's own funds. It may happen that an advantageous purchase could be made and an opportunity might be lost if your Company has no unissued capital . . . Banditry, which has cost the Company very dearly in life and expenditure of the Company's funds, seems to be dying out and it is hoped sincerely that 1959 will see the end of a distressing period for which I regret to say the immediate post-war Government of Great Britain must take the chief responsibility
. . .

1959. The capital of the company was increased from £565,000 to £805,500 in order to allow the acquisition of three other, smaller plantation rubber companies – Semenyih, Bukit and Tarun. This gave the Brooklands company a total acreage of 13,810, of which only 474 acres were not under rubber. The total crop for that year was over six million pounds. Total net current assets were £1,150,501, of which reserves represented £431,516. The profit after tax was £74,684, and a dividend of 35 per cent was paid. Douglas Money retires on attaining the age of seventy and offers himself for re-election, as does his son, J. K. Money.

Stockholders will doubtless have welcomed the proposals for the acquisition of three subsidiary Companies on terms which were worked out by all the Directors concerned to ensure that the only advantage lay in the improved marketability of shares combined, of course, with the spread of risks over a larger acreage. It may not be realised . . . that in tropical agriculture there are risks such as storm damage, plant diseases, insect pests, not to mention local strikes, although these, happily, are now less likely owing to intelligent co-operation between the Employers' Federation and the Trade Unions . . .

Much is being learnt to day regarding methods of increasing crop. Several forms of stimulation, including the application of synthetic compounds to the tapping surface . . . are widely used . . . The management of a Rubber Estate today calls for very

Douglas Money with son John and daughter-in-law, 1959.

much more knowledge and also for a higher degree of intelligence than was the case in the early days of rubber planting, when skilled management of unhealthy and untrained Labour presented its own special problems. Today science has virtually eliminated malaria and other diseases which affected at least ninety per cent of all Labour employed on Rubber Estates. There is no longer any excuse for bad tapping, but planters are plagued by demands of bureaucracy which, alas, in conformity with Parkinson's law, exhibits the same fecundity well known in these Islands . . .

1960. In this year the Kuala Pertang Syndicate was acquired. This added another 5,400 acres, of which 2,837 were under rubber, to the company's holdings, which now amounted to 19,210 acres. The profit after tax was £207,317, and a dividend of 60 per cent was paid. The accounting period, however, was eighteen months because of the need to amalgamate the accounts of the various companies.

The Rubber Plantation Industry is facing a period of reduced earnings, due mainly to competition with synthetics which now compete in the world's markets with our product, both from the price angle and increasingly on a quality basis . . . Today plantation grades are only used by manufacturers as and when it is advantageous for them to employ such grades, either because they are cheaper or because they believe that a blend of synthetic and plantation will produce a better product in a fiercely competitive market . . .

Assuming always that profits can be earned by the production of plantation rubber, an important issue is the amount of taxation which is levied on the Industry by the Governments of those countries where the rubber tree flourishes. It would be invidious to draw attention to the risks that are run by investors in certain tropical countries, and it is hardly necessary for me to point out that attractive as penal taxation may appear the risk of overdoing it can bring very unpleasant consequences when the goose refuses, or is unable to lay any more golden eggs . . . Looking to the future, and in spite of all the developments in the realm of synthetics, there appears to be a future for plantation rubber in a country which has a stable government and no racial problems which must bedevil the growing of rubber in other and less fortunate parts of the world . . .

1961. The profit after tax was £119,217, and a dividend of 20 per cent was paid.

Future prospects . . . cannot be assessed without indulgence in a certain amount of guesswork. Broadly speaking the Industry is looking forward to a time when high yielding clonal rubber will be in full bearing over a substantial part of those rubber plantations which have been able to eliminate low yielding areas. There is, today, evidence that on suitable land, rubber plantations will harvest between 1,500 and 2,000 lbs per acre. On such a yield basis . . . plantation rubber should more than hold its own in the world's markets . . .

The old Brooklands Estate comprises flat alluvial land where it is relatively difficult to obtain high yields. In the past, skilled management and healthy conditions for labour counter-balanced relatively lower yields, but today improved conditions on hilly estates (formerly malarious) not to mention Trade Union activities, have deprived large areas of alluvial land of their competitive advantages, and there is a growing tendency in such areas to substitute for rubber the cultivation of oil palms . . .

I visited all the estates of the Group . . . and, although conditions in Malaya are very different from those that prevailed prior to the last war, it was pleasant to find a spirit of optimism among present-day planters . . .

1962. The profit after tax was £95,016, and a dividend of 17½ per cent was paid.

1963. The profit for the year after tax was £91,980, and a dividend of 17½ per cent was paid.

Propaganda in aid of new and extended uses for plantation rubber of all kinds is no longer fashionable, and the Industry as a whole is pinning its faith upon the production of rubber at lower cost as the main means of salvation. Unfortunately, the Industry has had to face recently increased wage demands by Labour which, had they been met by the rubber producers, would have caused complete breakdown throughout Malaya, which depends very largely upon the profitability of rubber growing. During the negotiations facts must have demonstrated that the workers were in no way suffering from low wages or long hours, and that in all probability no other country in the world could show so great an improvement in the standard of living over the past twenty-five years. At this stage in this history of the Industry it would have been madness for those responsible on both sides to have allowed the plantation workers to wreck the Industry, and leave themselves to face an existence only paralleled in the poorer parts of India . . . As evidence of goodwill towards the workers, and although it is not yet possible to ascertain exactly what unemployment may result, a substantial increase in the standard wage had been granted, and the future for large areas of old seedling rubber remains doubtful.

1964. The profit for the year after tax was £105,460, and a dividend of 20 per cent was paid.

The threat of Socialist legislation, including an unknown Capital Gains Tax, led to a professional report being made on the Company's properties, with a view to ascertaining whether any of the Estates had development potential for anything other than the growing of tropical produce. The possibility of the Estates being more valuable through their suitability for housing development or mineral production was investigated, and the report recently received from an independent Valuer indicated that none of the Company's Estates, with the exception of a dozen or so acres, had any such development potential in the foreseeable future . . .

Politically the Company is menaced by two confrontations. In Malaysia there is Indonesian aggression, and at home we have a Hungarian economic theory embodied in a Finance Bill which might well have been designed to damage this country's economy, not by intention, but by sheer economic ignorance. There is an old saying that in business rogues and fools are the chief dangers but that the latter do most damage. It is a pity that the present Government finds that liberal socialism does not appeal to the debased kind of voter and has tried to gain political popularity by attacking the business world which alone can provide the subsidies and free gifts beloved by Left Wing socialism . . .

The Final Phase

We have come to that go-go period of British history when the political asset-strippers in Transport House and the financial ones in the City contrived, between them, to change the geography of British industry. The plantation companies appeared as almost inevitable victims. Politically unpopular as tangible evidence of a colonial past everyone was trying to forget, heavily taxed in two countries, exposed to increasing pressures to become either 'Malayanised' or nationalised, they no longer attracted the young men who once had left Britain in order to farm the world. On the other hand, they did attract the financial wide boys looking for a cheap buy and a quick strip. As the previous pages have shown, their capital structure and their share values seldom represented very accurately their asset values. Their varying fortunes in the past had classified them as speculative investments. Their obvious lack of any settled future as sterling companies in former colonial territories did nothing to add to their value as investments. Yet, as has been seen, wise management had not only ensured that their break-up value would be considerably more than their market value, but also had, if the management had been as prudent as Douglas Money's always was, left them sitting on considerable cash reserves. Moreover, if they were operating in Malaya, where there was still a market economy and a capitalist system, there would be ready buyers among the Malayan and Chinese entrepreneurs for whatever an asset-stripper might want to sell.

Douglas had experienced some of the dangers of the situation as chairman of what had been a failing plantation company before he tried to rescue it. That attempt had led him to a hard-fought but inevitable defeat. He described the situation with his customary clarity when he reported to the Annual General Meeting of that particular company in 1964:

On current profit figures, and even more so on our dividend record, it has not been surprising that the market price of the shares on the London Stock Exchange remained for so long at around 6d. per share, which represented substantially less than the value of the Estates. This of course drew the attention of intelligent investors to this Company, and in September last, an American citizen visited Malaya where he showed an interest in the Estates. A substantial block of the Company's shares changed hands at that time, and it is significant that the market price has more than doubled in a short period.

Recently your Board received a communication indicating that this American and two of his friends wished to join the Board and Resolutions to this effect may be proposed at the Annual General Meeting. The absence of any reason given for this request brings to mind an operation which was popular some years ago, when speculators acquired control of Plantation Companies, after which the Estates were disposed of as speedily as possible and without regard to the potential or true value of the properties.

It should be pointed out that the maximum number of Directors is limited to five by the Articles of Association, and therefore any three Directors could dispose of the estate without reference to the wishes of the shareholders, so in the absence of any declared intention by the American gentleman and his friends, it becomes impossible for your Board to recommend the shareholders to vote for any appointment which could lead to a fundamental change in the present policy of your Company . . .

He had described the position accurately, and things happened almost exactly as he suggested they might happen. This, however, had always been a failing company, and it was not one that he had formed and led from its beginnings. But when there was a suggestion that another, and more powerful group might be attempting to take over the companies he had devoted most of his life to leading out of successive crises towards success, then it became obvious to him that his last duty to them was to rescue them. If he could bring them all together – Brooklands, Henrietta, Chambong and Kampong Kuantan – into a single company, then it would be large enough and powerful enough to resist being broken up.

In a circular to all the shareholders in all the four companies he said:

The Directors of the four Companies have agreed proposals for the merger of those Companies through the medium of a new holding company named Plantation Holdings Ltd . . . Your Boards have for some time felt that a merger would be a logical and desirable step from the point of view of each of the Companies. We therefore requested Baring Brothers to formulate terms upon which such a merger might be carried out and the proposals now agreed by us are in accordance with their advice . . .

The creation of a holding company will enable the pooled cash resources of the Group to be more efficiently used and facilitate much closer co-operation between all of the Companies . . . Ordinary Stockholders will become members of a single and larger company whose shares should be more freely marketable and have a higher investment status . . . Your Boards consider it most desirable that Malaysian participation in the plantation industry of that country should be encouraged, as should the appointment of Malaysians to executive positions . . . It will also be the policy of the Board of the new holding company to expand its interests as and when suitable opportunities arise . .

It was in this way that a new holding company was started, and it is here that this book finishes. It would be right, however, to quote the closing passages of Douglas's last address to the shareholders as chairman of the company he had formed to hold together the plantations that had been his life interest:

On a personal note, you will notice in the circular that we sent out that this will be the last Meeting at which I shall have the privilege of addressing you from the Chair. I have expressed the view that once the Company was going along well as the result of the amalgamation, I did not wish to hold on to the helm and would be happy to retire in due course.

I feel now that, if this Resolution is passed today, I can safely leave the Chair and it will be up to you to decide whether I have done my duty by you or not. I definitely feel that I am entitled to retire – I am old enough to get out, I hope to remain a Director of the parent company for some time and I am still a Director of numerous subsidiaries and I will be able to keep in touch with the eastern areas very, very happily . . .

MR CORK. Mr Chairman, before you go, I think after many years officiating on the Boards of rubber companies it may be as you said, that you will not do it again. I think that we will all regret the passing from our midst of a personality such as Mr Money. He has been forthright – sometimes he agrees with shareholders and sometimes he disagrees with shareholders – but, in either event, he makes that perfectly clear. I would like, and I am sure Shareholders will feel today, that they would like to show their appreciation for the many years of service you have given to this industry by the usual method. (Applause).

THE CHAIRMAN. Mr Cork, ladies and gentlemen, I thank you very much for your very kind expression.

MR CORK. One last point, Mr Chairman. It appears that you did not actually declare the Resolution carried. For your final going-out job would you do that?

THE CHAIRMAN. I thought I had done that. I said it was 'carried unanimously', but perhaps I did not make it plain enough. Anyway, for the purpose of keeping the Minutes in order, I have great pleasure in declaring that this resolution has been carried nem. con.

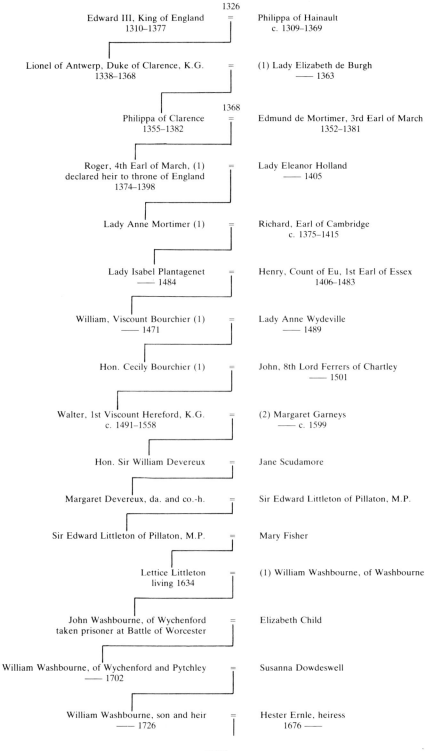

1326
Edward III, King of England   =   Philippa of Hainault
1310–1377   c. 1309–1369

Lionel of Antwerp, Duke of Clarence, K.G.   =   (1) Lady Elizabeth de Burgh
1338–1368   —— 1363

1368
Philippa of Clarence   =   Edmund de Mortimer, 3rd Earl of March
1355–1382   1352–1381

Roger, 4th Earl of March, (1)   =   Lady Eleanor Holland
declared heir to throne of England   —— 1405
1374–1398

Lady Anne Mortimer (1)   =   Richard, Earl of Cambridge
c. 1375–1415

Lady Isabel Plantagenet   =   Henry, Count of Eu, 1st Earl of Essex
—— 1484   1406–1483

William, Viscount Bourchier (1)   =   Lady Anne Wydeville
—— 1471   —— 1489

Hon. Cecily Bourchier (1)   =   John, 8th Lord Ferrers of Chartley
—— 1501

Walter, 1st Viscount Hereford, K.G.   =   (2) Margaret Garneys
c. 1491–1558   —— c. 1599

Hon. Sir William Devereux   =   Jane Scudamore

Margaret Devereux, da. and co.-h.   =   Sir Edward Littleton of Pillaton, M.P.

Sir Edward Littleton of Pillaton, M.P.   =   Mary Fisher

Lettice Littleton   =   (1) William Washbourne, of Washbourne
living 1634

John Washbourne, of Wychenford   =   Elizabeth Child
taken prisoner at Battle of Worcester

William Washbourne, of Wychenford and Pytchley   =   Susanna Dowdeswell
—— 1702

William Washbourne, son and heir   =   Hester Ernle, heiress
—— 1726   1676 ——

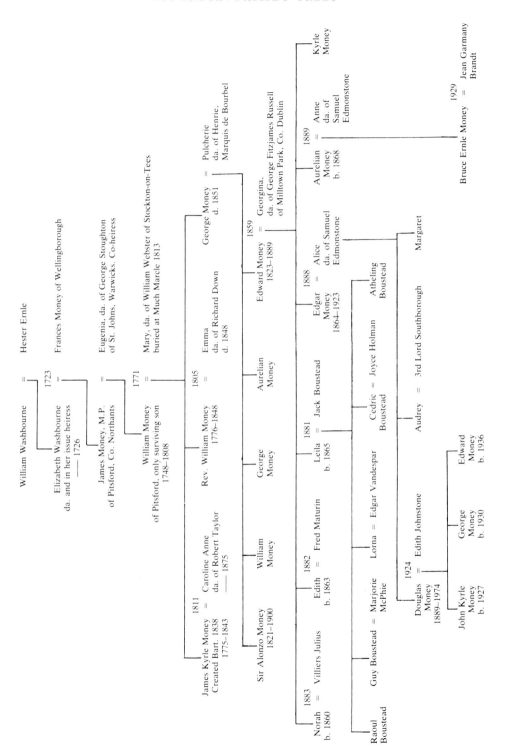

William Washbourne = Hester Ernle
                1723

Elizabeth Washbourne = Frances Money of Wellingborough
da. and in her issue heiress
        — 1726

James Money, M.P. = Eugenia, da. of George Stoughton
of Pitsford, Co. Northants   of St. Johns, Warwicks. Co-heiress

William Money = Mary, da. of William Webster of Stockton-on-Tees
of Pitsford, only surviving son   buried at Much Marcle 1813
1748–1808
        1771

Rev. William Money = Emma
1776–1848   da. of Richard Down
                d. 1848
        1805

George Money = Pulcherie
d. 1851   da. of Henrie,
         Marquis de Bourbel

Edward Money = Georgina,
1823–1889   da. of George Fitzjames Russell
         of Milltown Park, Co. Dublin
        1859

Kyrle
Money

Aurelian = Anne
Money   da. of
b. 1868   Samuel
         Edmonstone
        1889

Bruce Ernle Money = Jean Garmany
                Brandt
        1929

James Kyrle Money = Caroline Anne
Created Bart. 1838   da. of Robert Taylor
1775–1843   — 1875
        1811

George   William   Aurelian
Money   Money   Money

Sir Alonzo Money
1821–1900

Edgar = Alice
Money   da. of Samuel
1864–1923   Edmonstone
        1888

Atheling
Boustead

Cedric = Joyce Holman
Boustead

Margaret

Audrey = 3rd Lord Southborough

Leila = Jack Boustead
b. 1865
        1881

Edith = Fred Maturin
b. 1863
        1882

Lorna = Edgar Vandespar

Norah = Villiers Julius
b. 1860
        1883

Guy Boustead = Marjorie
            McPhie

Raoul
Boustead

Douglas = Edith Johnstone
Money
1889–1974
        1924

John Kyrle   George   Edward
Money   Money   Money
b. 1927   b. 1930   b. 1936

Index

compiled by Valerie Lewis Chandler, B.A., A.L.A.A. March 1979.